THE FORCE OF
VOCATION

THE FORCE OF VOCATION

THE LITERARY CAREER OF

Adele

WISEMAN

RUTH PANOFSKY

UNIVERSITY OF MANITOBA PRESS

© 2006 Ruth Panofsky

University of Manitoba Press
Winnipeg, Manitoba R3T 2N2 Canada
www.umanitoba.ca/uofmpress

Printed in Canada on acid-free paper by Friesens.

Cover and text design: Doowah Design
Cover photograph: Amy Zahl
Spine photograph: Douglas Barnaby

Library and Archives Canada Cataloguing in Publication
Panofsky, Ruth
    The force of vocation : the literary career of Adele
    Wiseman / Ruth Panofsky.

Includes bibliographical references and index.
ISBN 0-88755-689-2

    1. Wiseman, Adele, 1928–1992—Criticism and
    interpretation. 2. Novelists, Canadian (English)—20th
    century—Biography. I. Title.

PS8545.I85Z74 2006   C813'.54
C2006-901551-1

The University of Manitoba gratefully acknowledges the
financial support for its publication program provided by
the Government of Canada through the Book Publishing
Industry Development Program (BPIDP), the Canada Council
for the Arts, the Manitoba Arts Council, and the Manitoba
Department of Culture, Heritage and Tourism.

For my mother,
Brenda Yampolsky Panofsky,
and in memory of my grandmother,
Lily Freder Yampolsky

Table of Contents

THIS BOOK FOCUSSES ON ADELE WISEMAN, a seminal figure in Canadian letters who, over the course of a life, engaged with other writers, literary agents, editors, and publishers. Wiseman figures throughout this work as a public author, defined by publishing scholar James West as a "serious literary artist who meant also to reach a large audience through the publishing apparatus of the time and who wanted to earn a living by writing."1 In appraising Wiseman's career and studying her role in the public realms of publishing practice and literary reception, I highlight her vocational and material contribution to literary culture in Canada during the latter half of the twentieth century.

This study eschews the romantic fantasy of the naturally talented author who descends from on high to disseminate her writerly gifts. It posits Wiseman as a writer who, for better or worse, charted the course of her writing life as she doggedly and ambitiously perfected her craft, sought a wide audience for her work, and cleaved to the high moral value she attributed to her writing. In large part, the aim of this work is to identify the author's artistic agency in negotiating the terms of her literary career.

This book offers an empirical account of a literary career that spanned forty years. It responds to the call of eminent critics, among them Frank Davey, who has noted that the

> empirical study of twentieth-century English-Canadian publishing is extremely scant. Autobiographies by bookmen like John Gray [of the Macmillan Company of Canada] and Lorne Pierce [of Ryerson Press] offer little detail about relations between author and publisher, or about publishing and marketing practices; the few biographies of twentieth-century authors often have had surprisingly little to say about how a book came to be published, on what contractual terms, with what influence by the publisher, or about what sales ensued.[2]

Although numerous biographies of twentieth-century Canadian authors have appeared since 1988, when Davey lamented the dearth of information available about the publishing side of writers' lives, few describe the professional experience of authorship. For the most part, recent biographies continue to emphasize writers' private lives and personal relationships.[3]

In light of the available resources held in archival repositories in Canada and elsewhere, the lack of interest in author-publisher relations, publishing practice, and literary reception remains puzzling and points to a potential bias on the part of literary scholars and historians—those scholars most likely to write literary biographies—in favour of studying the personal over the professional side of authors' lives. As book historian Francess Halpenny has acknowledged, however, challenges still "abound in accounting, on the basis of research, for the *histoire* of Canadian books, for the past development and present state of the Canadian book trade, for the place of the book in Canadian society."[4] Difficult as these challenges might be—the tasks of locating archival holdings relevant to one's subject of inquiry, of gaining access to restricted archival material, of securing permission to cite from unpublished archival sources, for example—they are not insurmountable. Moreover, if they are met, as Halpenny further advocates, "we shall know much more about how the passage from author to reader has occurred in Canada and has created our literary history."[5]

In a 2002 article, critic Travis DeCook urged literary scholars to concentrate "on the institutions that mediate our engagement with literature. . . . [since] any understanding of literary history should take into account the institutions and economic forces involved with canonicity."[6] Today, the history of publishing in Canada, which has shaped our literary history and its culture of authorship, is an emerging field of study. As literary critic Carole Gerson maintains, a knowledge of publishing history "is still a significant gap in the perspective of many scholars."[7] Gerson articulates "the need to examine more fully the structural factors governing the creation of Canadian literary culture,"[8] and asserts the corollary need for research on publishers' archives as cultural repositories.

Gerson endorses critic Wayne Templeton's analogy of publishers as "architects of culture" and his compelling argument that

> [a] study of publishing in Canada is not so much a survey of Canadian publishing as a statement on Canadian culture, of which publishing, writing, and national self-awareness become points of a vital triangle of mediation with publishing at the apex. A nation's self-awareness, in the cultural context, is created by writers . . . a nation's literature in turn is created by publishers.[9]

Scholars and critics have begun the exciting and necessary work toward building an understanding of Canadian publishing practice and the importance of publishers as cultural workers. The groundbreaking, three-volume *History of the Book in Canada*, for example, charts the historical development to 1980 of literary culture and authorship in Canada. Roy MacSkimming's *The Perilous Trade* surveys Canadian English-language publishing houses of the twentieth century; there are brief histories of English publishing in Québec and of the literary House of Anansi Press; and the enterprising Harlequin is the subject of a book-length study. Books by James King and Sam Solecki celebrate publisher Jack McClelland and his dedication to issuing the work of Canadian writers.

Several scholars have studied the literary careers of Canadian authors. Nick Mount and Clarence Karr, respectively, examine the publishing careers of late nineteenth-century and popular early twentieth-century Canadian writers, including Nellie McClung, L.M. Montgomery, and Arthur Stringer, and JoAnn McCaig analyzes the international success of short story writer Alice Munro in the context of her relationships with mentor Robert Weaver of the CBC and literary agent Virginia Barber of New York. Recently, the scholarly journal *Studies in Canadian Literature* devoted a special issue to "Canadian Literature and the Business of Publishing."[10] I have been much influenced by current writing on literary publishing in Canada and author-publisher relations by scholars such as Gwendolyn Davies, Carole Gerson, Janet B. Friskney, Clarence Karr, George L. Parker, Carl Spadoni, and Bruce Whiteman. These writers have helped me better understand the interconnection between publishing practice and authorship.

This examination of Adele Wiseman's literary career aims to underscore the importance of publishing to Canada's cultural enterprise, to contribute to the literary and cultural record of this country, and to emphasize that cultural identity is conceived and created not just by artists and writers but also by those who publish their work. I contend, like Francess Halpenny, that to "fully understand the literary career of any author . . . [we must know] the publishing history of that author's works (sometimes a curious story for Canadian writers) and the effect of this history not only upon the author's public success and literary reputation but even upon the writing style."[11] Wiseman's work had an international reach. It was issued by major publishing houses in Canada, the United States, and Great Britain, and her connections with prominent editors and publishers make a study of her literary career especially compelling. This consideration of Wiseman's career as a writer was conceived as a deliberate challenge to critics who dismiss an author whose later work did not enjoy the success of her first novel. In asserting Wiseman's importance—she remains one of Canada's foremost writers of the modern period—I am not avowing that she received the same degree of public recognition as her contemporary Margaret Laurence, for example. I am arguing, however, that she enjoyed an early success in 1956 with the publication of *The Sacrifice* that confirmed her status as an author, and that throughout her life she regarded herself—as did other writers, literary agents, editors, and publishers—as accomplished. My objective is not to study Wiseman as a neglected writer, but rather to reassess and broaden the parameters of her career beyond the traditional critical focus on her award-winning novel *The Sacrifice*.

The course of Wiseman's career can be read as the progressive loss of readership and literary recognition, with little economic gain over a lifetime. To explain this pattern of career development, this study underscores Wiseman's responses to key events in her writerly life. Rather than speculate as to the psychological motivation for her career decisions, I interpret those decisions through the lens of the public record available in archival collections, interviews, and other primary and secondary material that help elucidate the author's career choices. In this study of Wiseman's literary career, I hesitate to privilege psychological interpretation, which may be subjective, over empirical, evidentiary analysis. One psychological rationalization might suggest, for example, that Wiseman was overwhelmed by the triumph of her first novel and that her subsequent career decisions reflected a general ambivalence over early success. This study confirms that Wiseman was a dynamic personality, that she was often stubborn and sometimes naïve, but, for the most part, it leaves the task of psychological interpretation to the future biographer whose attention to the individual's private life should render an intriguing portrait of the author. Instead, this book investigates the public side of the writer's life and shows Wiseman to be deliberate and thoughtful about her work, a wilful navigator among literary agents, editors, and publishers, and the most generous of literary mentors.

The organizing structure of this volume, around Wiseman's publications, her writerly relationships, and related activities, is not strictly chronological. For this reason, I include a detailed chronology of Wiseman's life and an appendix listing her principal publications as aids to the reader.

I have made extensive use of archival and primary sources. An invaluable repository of information is the forty-year correspondence between Adele Wiseman and Margaret Laurence, held in the Adele Wiseman fonds and the Margaret Laurence fonds, Clara Thomas Archives, Scott Library, York University. Although Wiseman's letters to Laurence prior to 1962 are not available, it is possible to extrapolate from Laurence's side of their correspondence a sense of Wiseman's activities between 1947 and 1961. I also draw on the incomparable resources available in key archival collections, most notably the Clarke, Irwin and Company Limited fonds; the Macmillan Company of Canada fonds; the McClelland and Stewart Ltd. fonds; and the

Jack McClelland fonds, all housed at the William Ready Division of Archives and Research Collections, McMaster University Library; the Malcolm Ross fonds, Special Collections, University of Calgary Library, as well as the Malcolm Ross Papers, Thomas Fisher Rare Book Library, University of Toronto; and the Margaret Laurence fonds and the Adele Wiseman fonds, Clara Thomas Archives, Scott Library, York University. Interviews with individuals who knew Wiseman also have aided my efforts to chart the development of one of Canada's most influential writers.

In this study of Wiseman as public author, I do not include her works that remain unpublished. The Adele Wiseman fonds held at York University includes, among other work, two plays, numerous essays, several children's stories, and hundreds of poems that exist outside the purview of this book. Some of the archival material is closed to researchers, and permission to cite from previously unpublished material held in the Wiseman fonds is difficult to secure. As a result, scholars are prevented from examining and citing archival sources that might, at some future date, prove relevant to a study of authorship such as that presented here.[12]

This book is the result of generous support and invaluable cooperation. First, I would like to express my sincere gratitude to the Canada Council for a Professional Writer's Grant in support of my work on Adele Wiseman. I am grateful to Ryerson University for providing generous research funding in aid of this project. As well, I wish to thank the anonymous reviewers whose detailed and enthusiastic comments helped sharpen the focus and structure of this volume.

For permission to cite from archival collections held at the William Ready Division of Archives and Research Collections, McMaster University Library, I thank Clarke, Irwin; the Macmillan Company of Canada; McClelland and Stewart; and the late Jack McClelland. For permission to cite from the Curtis Brown Ltd. archives and the Oral History Research Collection, I thank the Rare Book and Manuscript Library of Columbia University. I am indebted to Robert Weaver for allowing me to cite from his papers held at Library and Archives Canada.

I welcome this opportunity to acknowledge the invaluable assistance provided by Carl Spadoni, William Ready Division of Archives and Research Collections, McMaster University Library; Debbie Brentnell and Anne Goddard, Library and Archives Canada; Apollonia Lang Steele, Special Collections, University of Calgary Library; Lewis Stubbs and Shelley Sweeney, Archives and Special Collections, University of Manitoba Library; Suzanne Dubeau, Michael Moir, Sean Smith, and the late Kent Haworth, Clara Thomas Archives, Scott Library, York University; the staff of the Thomas Fisher Rare Book Library, University of Toronto; and Bernard Crystal, Rare Book and Manuscript Library, Columbia University.

I wish to thank the following individuals for graciously allowing me to quote from personal and telephone interviews: Kildare Dobbs, Miriam Dorn, Sharon Drache, Phyllis Grosskurth, Christina Kurata, John Pearce, Sidney Perlmutter, Janis Rapoport, the late Mordecai Richler, Chava Rosenfarb, the late Malcolm Ross, Kenneth Sherman, the late John Speers, Richard Teleky, and Robert Weaver.

Many others also have helped with this project, and I am pleased to take this occasion to thank them for their generous assistance and encouragement: Abe Arnold, Margaret Atwood, Jeffrey Berlin, Michael Brown, Barbara Craig, Antonio D'Alfonso, Jack David, Mary Jane Edwards, Janet B. Friskney, Adam Fuerstenberg, Carole Gerson, Douglas Gibson, Elizabeth Greene, Michael Greenstein, Leslie Howsam, Sharon Katz, James King, David Laurence, Jocelyn Laurence, Marcia Mack, Seymour Mayne, Bruce Meyer, Pamela Milne, Goldie Morgentaler, Sylvia Ostry, Mary Perlmutter, Jim Polk, Joe Rosenblatt,

Dmitry Stone, Tamara Stone, the late Miriam Waddington, and Maurice Yeates. John Lennox and Clara Thomas have been especially encouraging of my work on Wiseman. I also appreciate the support of my colleagues in the Cultural Studies Working Group of Ryerson University: John Cook, Dennis Denisoff, Michael Finn, Kathleen Kellett-Betsos, Karen Mulhallen, and Monique Tschofen.

For research assistance I owe a special thanks to the indefatigable Heather Milne, whose critical insight helped shape this project, and for expert advice and practical guidance throughout the writing of this book I am indebted to Donez Xiques. I am deeply grateful to David Carr, Director of the University of Manitoba Press, for his interest in Adele Wiseman and his commitment to this project, and to Managing Editor Patricia Sanders for her editorial acumen. Finally, I extend warm appreciation to my husband, Gary Gottlieb, and our children, Bram and Liza, for embracing Adele Wiseman, whose spirit has lived among us for many years.

Early versions of portions of this book appeared in *Room of One's Own* (1993); *We Who Can Fly: Poems, Essays and Memories in Honour of Adele Wiseman*, edited by Elizabeth Greene (1997); and *English Studies in Canada* (2001). Also, summary versions of several chapters were presented at the Association of Canadian College and University Teachers of English; the Society for the History of Authorship, Reading and Publishing; and the Society for Textual Scholarship.

THE FORCE OF
VOCATION

In 1956, AT THE AGE OF TWENTY-EIGHT, Adele Wiseman published *The Sacrifice*, a first novel that received international acclaim and established her reputation as a writer highly regarded for her moral vision, refined style, and authentic characters. Throughout her career, in works that grew increasingly complex in form and content, Wiseman struggled to articulate her place in history. Not surprisingly, given her driving ambition and writerly commitment to the Jewish immigrant experience, she found the struggle both rewarding and difficult. The child of immigrants from Russia, Wiseman regarded herself as a privileged Canadian writer, due, in no small part, to her parents' sacrifice and encouragement.

As she wrote in her *Memoirs*, Adele Wiseman believed that Canadian citizenship afforded her the "privilege" of "mobility and freedom"[1] that was not available to American women writers of her generation who faced an entrenched "male literary establishment" (58). When, as a youth, she made the commitment to become a writer, Wiseman felt comfortable doing so in a country that was coming of age and where "women writers have tended to write not with the hope of achieving equality, but in the assumption of at least equality" (45).

That a young Wiseman felt herself equal to the task of becoming a writer of significance signals the degree of confidence and commitment that later characterized her career. That she envisaged the possibility of achieving success as a Canadian writer shows that she—a child of immigrants who wrote about the immigrant experience—recognized Canada as home and hoped to contribute to its burgeoning cultural life. Wiseman's youthful optimism about her country and her future was not unfounded. Post-war Winnipeg promised new opportunities for young men and women alike. At the University of Manitoba, for example, where she studied as an undergraduate from 1945 to 1949, her efforts to become a writer were encouraged by professors and fellow students. Much later, Wiseman would describe her position as a writer: "I am [not] by any means the first or the most noteworthy woman writer in Canada, but . . . I stand historically at a kind of watershed, as possibly the first of the Canadian women prose writers, in English, to emerge after the Second World War" (45).

Although she knew herself to be Canadian by birth, Wiseman felt differentiated from mainstream culture and she perceived the world and the books she read through the dual, conflicted lens of a Jewish female. As an adolescent, she intuited that the "girls and women I read about in books were usually quite other than what I knew myself and the girls and women I knew to be" (16). Wiseman grew up during the Second World War and was deeply affected by Hitler's efforts to eradicate the Jewish population of Europe. As she matured, her identity as a Jew strengthened:

> [T]here was very little of innocence about the world into
> which I emerged as a young adult. We were counting
> our dead. The Second World War had ended. We had,

technically, been on the winning side. We felt a great relief, though there was little cause for euphoria. Whatever
the relief that was felt by everyone else that the war was
over and a way of life had been preserved, for me, as a
Jew, I knew that not only a way of life but life itself had
been preserved. And so it was even a kind of rebirth. But
it was a rebirth that carried with it responsibility. In the
counting of our dead I had more dead than I could ever
count. . . . I did not feel guilt because I survived; I felt
the responsibility, rather, in some sense to make the dead
survive through me. (49)

Writing in the shadow of the Holocaust, as well as her own family
history, Wiseman envisaged the author as a moral witness to her time
and, in practice, became a "responsible" writer. As a novice writer,
when she began work on *The Sacrifice*, and throughout her career, she
wrote always as a Canadian, a woman, and a Jew who sought to explore the human condition. Attuned to historical pain as it translates
into the pain of everyday life, Wiseman unveiled the dynamics of a
cultural reality that most readers did not know and drew characters
who invariably "demand[ed] their dignity from brute reality" (27).

Wiseman later admitted, "In my own work, which has for me the
force of vocation, to aim for other than the highest would be not only
self-destructive but worse, boring. To aim for and miss the highest is
only failure. Not to aim for the highest is betrayal" (29). Much earlier,
as a young woman, Wiseman determined that she "would repay the
world for indulging me by writing great works, revealing itself to
itself" (52).

These telling statements articulate Wiseman's commitment to her
craft and the vocation of writer. Throughout her career, during successes and setbacks, Wiseman did not relinquish the task she set herself:

to write with power and insight, to consider important subjects, and to make a difference through her work. These were high standards, however, and Wiseman often was frustrated in her ability to satisfy her own aspirations and the requirements of agents, editors, and publishers.

This study analyzes the significant events and literary connections that marked Wiseman's career as a writer: the writing, publication, and reception of *The Sacrifice*, *Crackpot*, and *Old Woman at Play*; her relationships with literary agents, editors, and publishers; and her seminal experiences first as protege and later as friend and mentor to other writers. It follows the trajectory of Wiseman's career, from the soaring heights of early success—the ready acceptance of *The Sacrifice* by Macmillan of Canada, for example—to the mixed reception of her later work—such as the hesitant response of readers to the groundbreaking *Old Woman at Play*. Further, it suggests that Wiseman acted with self-conscious artistic agency throughout the course of her career. Her confidence in the face of conflict and a certainty in her position as author derived from an uncompromising view of the moral value and high seriousness of her work. That view of her work was also the cause of much conflict, however.

Wiseman's decision to become a writer was made at a young age. Without regard for economic gain, she set out to write of a world that had proven itself heartless and brutal. When, after a long literary apprenticeship and years of work, *The Sacrifice* received international acclaim as a mature and moving first novel, Wiseman earned the recognition and respect—in the form of positive reviews, prestigious literary awards, and a wide readership—coveted by authors and publishers alike.

Wiseman was a fortunate first-time novelist, for she acquired the recognition necessary to fuel her career. Her triumph at the age of twenty-eight reinforced a belief in herself as a pure writer, one who wrote for the sake of communicating her artistic vision. She was convinced she could continue writing for an established audience and that her efforts would be rewarded. Moreover, the success of *The Sacrifice*, profound as it was, influenced her choice of future projects and secured her publishers' good will and support throughout her career.

For her next project, Wiseman turned away from the novel and wrote a four-hour play entitled *The Lovebound: A Tragi-Comedy*, an undertaking that had an irrevocable impact on her career. Wiseman's publishers sought to dissuade her from writing a play; instead, they urged her to hone her ability as a novelist and begin a second work of fiction. Had another novel appeared soon after *The Sacrifice*—even if that hypothetical work had met with less success than her first novel—Wiseman likely would have retained her wide audience. Early achievement, however, convinced Wiseman that she ought to follow her own authorial instincts.

Wiseman's instincts shaped a literary career that did not unfold as a series of incremental successes. As the agent at the centre of her life's work, she held steadfast to a belief in the moral value of her writing and refused to concede to a market-driven model for her career. Hence, having written a strong first novel, she sought to challenge herself by writing a play. Whether the play would prove economically viable did not concern Wiseman. Against the advice of her trusted publishers, she trusted herself to complete a project of her own choosing.

Wiseman's career path was determined by a number of factors. First, *The Sacrifice* launched her literary career and established a potential market for her subsequent work. In the wake of much success, however, Wiseman refused to consider the market conditions that govern the publishing industry and would not court readers with a second novel that might resemble the style of *The Sacrifice*. She believed, instead, in the singular integrity of each literary work.

Second, Wiseman's preference for unusual character and incident reflected her iconoclastic world view that challenged, among other

prevailing stereotypes, modern notions of the Jew, female sexuality
and desire, and the cultural value of art. After *The Sacrifice*, Wiseman
wrote of Hoda, obese Jewish prostitute, and her incestuous love for
her son; and of Chaika Waisman, maker of dolls out of household
scraps, and her folk wisdom. The biblical resonances of *The Sacrifice*,
its elegant structure, patriarchal world view, and focus on male characters appealed to a wide audience. Wiseman's subsequent work was
discursive and female-centred, showed compassion for unlikely female
characters, and attracted fewer readers.

Third, Wiseman's career was affected by a prolonged hiatus of eighteen years between publication of *The Sacrifice* and her second novel,
Crackpot. Wiseman had great difficulty placing her second work of
fiction. In 1974, *Crackpot* reintroduced readers to the award-winning
author of *The Sacrifice*, but Wiseman's new novel did not re-establish a
large audience for her work.

Finally, and perhaps most significant, is the fact that Wiseman acted
as the agent who decided the course of her career. Unwilling to jockey
"for the perks and male networkmanship" that she recognized as "part
of the successful literary life," Wiseman always acted on her belief
"that writing supremely well is all that counts" (57–58). With little
regard for market conditions, and often to her own economic detriment, she determined the books she would write and struggled to find
publishers to support her various projects. No doubt, had she elected
to build on her success as the promising author of *The Sacrifice*, her
career would have followed a less arduous course. Instead, Wiseman
chose to begin anew with each project, turning always to face the
challenges presented by unfamiliar genres. As she would admit later,
"I wanted to be an every-kind of writer, to write whatever I wanted
to say in whatever way was best for each particular work" (25–26).
The diversity of her writing is evident in her published oeuvre that
includes a tragic novel, a comic novel, a long essay, a work of life

writing, a collection of essays, several poems, and two children's books. Her unpublished oeuvre includes a long two-act play, a short three-act play, essays, book reviews, radio scripts, numerous children's stories, an operetta, and hundreds of poems.

Wiseman's career can be seen as an example of the potential conflict between the author who hungers "for the transcendant [sic], the revelatory" (27) and asserts a moral commitment to truth and excellence, and the economic concerns of literary agents, editors, and publishers for a work's market potential. In fact, the passage of Wiseman's career turned on the sustained view of herself as a serious writer, fiercely dedicated to her artistic vision and the craft of writing. Even when she had reason to think her work might not be published, Wiseman would assert an unshakeable belief in the integrity of her writing and resume her search for a publisher.

The force of Wiseman's integrity as an author and her sense of moral accountability—to her subject matter and her audience—drove the composition, publication, and subsequent success of her first novel. Throughout her career, Wiseman maintained a primary connection with her art and her work as a writer, and today her writing retains a power first evinced in 1956 upon publication of *The Sacrifice*. It is the nature of Wiseman's work as an author that forms the subject of this book.

ONE

An Achieved Success

ADELE WISEMAN'S LITERARY CAREER began with a flourish. When *The Sacrifice* was published in 1956, seven years following its conception, it brought Wiseman widespread media attention and critical acclaim. The twenty-eight-year-old author was lauded in Canada, the United States, and Great Britain for her obvious talent and craft, which were viewed as remarkable for a first-time novelist. The combination of youth, fine intelligence, and precocious ability as a writer struck a chord that resonated with reviewers of *The Sacrifice*. Moreover, reviewers were engaged by the patriarchal context of a novel that encouraged empathy for Abraham, the murderer protagonist, while it discouraged compassion for Laiah, his victim.[1] The contemporary response to the novel shows the extent to which Wiseman's rise as writer was predicated upon admiration or "love"[2] for Abraham, felt powerfully and equally by the author and her first reviewers, who would overlook its "sacrifice" of a female character to affirm patriarchal order.

The Sacrifice was the work of a young woman who, early on, came to view herself as a writer and who created the opportunities necessary for serious and uninterrupted work. Wiseman's first novel tells the tragic story of Abraham's life in an unnamed city modelled after Wiseman's native Winnipeg. Having lost his two eldest sons in a pogrom, Abraham, his wife Sarah, and their remaining son Isaac flee the Ukraine and settle in the New World. As immigrants, the family members face new hardship in an unfamiliar environment. The novel charts their difficult adjustment to a strange culture, the clash of generations, and the crushing demise of a patriarch who cleaves to the notion that he is favoured by God as he murders Laiah, an open, sensual woman who misunderstands Abraham. The biblical story of Abraham and Isaac serves as shaping metaphor in a novel that focusses on modern Jewish experience and explores the haunting and abiding themes of morality, pride, and ambition.

Wiseman's childhood and youth in Winnipeg fed her imagination, nurtured her literary aspirations, and fostered the drive necessary to fulfil her ambition to become a writer. She once described the North End of Winnipeg where she was born (on 28 May 1928) and raised as "the very incubator of conflicting absolutes. I relate my tendency to go for broke, to try to make an equation for the secret of the universe every time I sit down to the typewriter, to my continuing need to make some kind of total sense of the complex environment of the Winnipeg I knew, the Noah's Ark of my childhood, the Tower of Babel of my adolescence."[3] Wiseman's parents and an infant sister, Miriam, left the Ukraine and arrived in Canada in 1923. After spending two years in Montreal, the family travelled west to Winnipeg, where they joined the large group of Jewish, German, Ukrainian, and Slavic immigrants who made their home in the North End of the city.

Pesach Waisman (later anglicized to Wiseman) had hoped to be a cantor, but on his father's death he had been apprenticed at the age of nine to his uncle, who was a tailor. Chaika Waisman (née Rosenberg) had been trained as a dressmaker. Both knew the adversity of living under constant threat of anti–Semitic attack. They had lived in Russia during the Tsarist era, had experienced famine, and had survived the First World War and the Russian Revolution. Like so many other immigrants, they sought a better life for themselves and their children in North America. Although they experienced hardship in Canada, they lived free of the threat of persecution and could educate their children as they wished. Raised in a secular, socialist environment, Wiseman always admired her parents, "working-class craftsmen"[4] who were affected by the Great Depression, which soon frustrated their desire and tremendous effort to establish themselves comfortably in Canada after they had finally left behind the daily trial of life in the Old World.

Pesach and Chaika Waisman set up a tailoring business, Inkster Tailors, and eventually purchased a home in Winnipeg's North End. During the most difficult years of the Second World War, they rented out their home while the family lived in quarters behind the tailoring shop. Later, when they returned to the house on Burrows Avenue, the Waismans rented out rooms to supplement their household income. Early on, Wiseman learned that misfortune was tempered by the devotion of family and the anodyne of books. As she explains in her *Memoirs*, "[b]ooks were a route into life and reality and simultaneously an escape from life and reality, from the searing quality of every moment of the raw-nerved child's encounters with existence."[5]

The Waismans chose to educate their four children first at the I.L. Peretz School, whose working-class and progressive character differed markedly from the traditional Jewish education offered at the Talmud Torah, and later in the public schools. The struggle to make a living in their tailoring business was fuelled by the hopes they harboured for their children's success.

Both Wiseman's parents, but her mother in particular, believed in "doing for the community."[6] Following the war in Europe, for example, an impoverished Chaika Waisman took into her home a Jewish orphan whom she raised as foster child.[7] Wiseman's *Old Woman at Play* describes her mother's craft of making dolls out of household scraps. These dolls Waisman distributed to needy children in and out of hospital.

Equally important were the other early lessons Wiseman learned from her mother. She inherited a love of words from Waisman, who kept her children

> on the long leash of an endless rope of language [her native Yiddish], looping and knotting us as firmly to her as ever she stitched edge to edge in a seam. She lassoed us daily and webbed us and gilded our lives with innumerable threads of prose. Words spun about us; sometimes the very air was afog with words that purled like a fine mist about our ears: stories and persuasions and fantasies and cajolings and adjurations and just plain fast-talking that fogged up your brain with ideas, intoxicated you, led you half-hypnotized where she wanted you to go.[8]

Waisman also taught her four children "to look up to what we would admire and not down to what would reduce us."[9] Wiseman's idealism—her belief that "I must proceed always as though what is conceivable may in some way become possible"[10]—derived in large part from her mother's counsel. Soon she understood that she was "duty bound to share"[11] her writing with the world, that art served as "communication, imitation, mediation, reorganization, re-creation, integration, innovation, interpretation, reconciliation, above all, as celebration."[12]

Not only did she heed Waisman by publishing her work, Wiseman passed on her mother's teaching to her own daughter. Tamara Stone, herself a painter and sculptor, recalls of her mother, Adele Wiseman:

> I was raised in the warm light of her conviction that we
> were exceptionally lucky, she and I, sharing the drive and
> the ability to make art. She taught me that this gift brings
> with it a responsibility to educate the world towards greater
> and more humane possibilities. . . . I want to continue my
> mother's work, building on what she learned and what I
> learned from her. . . . My mother felt that the very act of
> creating thoughtful art made better things possible.[13]

Wiseman's story of mentorship began with her mother and continues with her daughter, whose life and career are still unfolding. Her
experience of mentorship through her mother—unusual for women
of Wiseman's generation—fostered her aptitude for and delight in
nurturing creativity in others.

Like St. Urbain Street in Montreal, immortalized in large part by
Mordecai Richler as the former Jewish heart of that city, the North
End of Winnipeg now enjoys legendary status as the one-time centre
of Jewish life in the West. In an interview in 1999, Sidney Perlmutter,
a childhood friend of Wiseman and now emeritus professor of Radio
and Television Arts at Ryerson University in Toronto, described the
vibrant, equalizing character of the North End, where children were
sheltered from the real difficulties their parents faced, privilege was
unknown, and good times were abundant.[14] In an atmosphere that fed
the limitless possibilities of the imagination—despite limited funds
and a palpable marginalization—Wiseman flourished. Her parents
encouraged their daughter's bookishness, her independence, and her
unusual intellect. The public school system, where she often clashed
with her teachers, also served as catalyst to the young Wiseman.

Wiseman has described herself as "growing up just in time"[15] to
rescue the fictional representation of the Jew. If we are to accept the
description she provides in the essay "Memoirs of a Book-Molesting

Childhood"—and, in fact, in the artfulness of her essay collection of the same title, Wiseman embeds invaluable insight into her life and work—her apprenticeship as a reader was undertaken rather consciously. From her earliest recognition of "the mutual contamination of the lived life and the lived reading" (6), Wiseman would not separate reading from experience and soon grew into an "adversarial reader" (16). Frustrated, nay, appalled by the representation of Jewish characters and, later, female characters, she recalled "slamming the book on Sir Walter Scott: 'What REAL dark beautiful exotic Jewish maiden would fall for your wimpy knight?'" (17). Even in her youth, as she sped randomly across and through the local library's "Dr Dolittles, the Bobbsey (and other) Twins, the Oz books, Pooh, Heidi, the Swiss Family Robinson, the works of Louisa May Alcott, Gene Stratton Porter . . . L.M. Montgomery, and *Lorna Doone*" (11–12), romance novels, and *Huckleberry Finn*, Wiseman always read as a "Jewish child in the gentile world" (15). The experience of being "other"—in life and in reading—later found expression in Wiseman's own work where she could confront "that which pained and frightened" (26) her most. Both her novels, written as they are from the centre of a culture and a tradition, offer subversively nuanced views of the Jew in the latter half of the twentieth century.

Wiseman's experience of the public primary school system in Winnipeg's North End was an unsavoury contrast to home. Primary schools and secondary schools (to a lesser degree) often were alien environments where children of immigrants frequently were made to feel unwelcome. Under principal G.J. Reeve, however, the open, stimulating atmosphere of St. John's Technical High School, with its large number of Jewish students,[16] aroused Wiseman's ambition. Unlike many aspiring writers, she did not keep diaries or seek to imitate the work of others. She did make her own work public, however, by submitting a story to *Torch*, the high school yearbook that awarded her second prize in a short story contest. With Clarice Cohen, a literary friend, Wiseman also published a poem in *Torch*, whose grand, evocative stance suggested both her working-class roots and her literary aspirations. It began:

> Is it our fate to always be
> Suppressed beneath senility?
> How can we strive for greater things
> When held like puppets, worked with strings?[17]

Despite its curricular "rigidities,"[18] which often rankled the independently minded Wiseman, she left St. John's prepared to meet the challenges of undergraduate study at the University of Manitoba, where she enrolled in 1945 as a student of English and psychology.

Wiseman was fortunate in her choice of institution. In her first year of study, the University of Manitoba became the first Canadian university to remove admission quotas against Jews and other minority groups and the Faculty of Arts welcomed many Jewish students.[19] As an undergraduate, Wiseman published a critical study of the poetry of Gerard Manley Hopkins in *Creative Campus*, the university magazine. From 28 June to 13 September 1947, she wrote a regular column (filling in for Roland Penner, later the Attorney General of Manitoba) for the *Westerner*, a Winnipeg newspaper with communist sympathies. One of her stories, "Nor Youth Nor Age," was awarded the Chancellor's Prize and also appeared in *Creative Campus*. Not only was Wiseman a gifted writer—a fact her professors soon appreciated—she was a successful student who in 1946 won a Sellers Scholarship in Arts and a Delta Phi Epsilon Bursary.

In her first two years, Wiseman would have been taught poetry by Master's student John Speers, who went on to become an Anglican priest. In 1999, an elderly Speers remembered her fondly as "gamin-like, small, tomboyish, out for adventure, a very upbeat sort of person, brilliant, attractive, and such fun to be with."[20] Speers described Wiseman's essays as "beautifully written in crystalline prose." He also was invited to the Wiseman home to tutor her circle of literary friends in poetry, where he was drawn in by the seductive combination of stimulating discussion, a liberal atmosphere, and good food.

Another professor who became a mentor and lifelong friend was Malcolm Ross, who taught for five years at the University of Manitoba. Educated at the University of New Brunswick, the University of Toronto, and Cornell University, Ross enjoyed an illustrious career as literary scholar and professor of English—he taught at Indiana University, the University of Manitoba, Queen's University, the University of Toronto, and Dalhousie University—as editor of *Queen's Quarterly* (1953 to 1956), champion of Canadian literature, and, between 1958 and 1978, founding general editor of McClelland and Stewart's landmark New Canadian Library (NCL) paperback reprint series that fostered widespread interest in, and unprecedented respect for, Canadian literature. In 1978, when she celebrated NCL as "one of the most valuable, significant and far-reaching events in our literary history," Margaret Laurence acknowledged the debt of "future generations"[21] to Ross. Known for his "catholic approach to literature and criticism,"[22] Ross was a particular friend to aspiring writers whose work he sought to nourish with sensitive criticism and warm encouragement. As writer Robertson Davies would affirm, "Canadian writers have not had a better friend. . . . He's moderate, critical, sensible and not a crusader. There is nobody who does more, consistently, to encourage Canadian studies on a high level."[23]

Throughout her life, Wiseman sought Ross's careful response to each of her writing projects, including her unpublished plays and poems, and they continued a relationship that ended only with Wiseman's death in 1992. In a telephone interview in 1999, Ross

L to R: Adele Wiseman,
William Stobie,
Margaret Stobie,
7 October 1949, at
Wiseman's home,
490 Burrows Avenue,
Winnipeg.
(Archives and Special
Collections, University of
Manitoba Library)

described his long-time "paternal"[24] connection to Wiseman, which
also meant a great deal to his former student. Her "gratitude and love"
for her "patient mentor"[25] are evident in Wiseman's correspondence
with Ross, written throughout her life and held at the University of
Calgary Library and the Thomas Fisher Rare Book Library, University
of Toronto. With Ross, Wiseman was personal and confiding, at times
even more so than in extant letters to her peer Margaret Laurence,
with whom she shared an intimate friendship. She never felt, as Diana
Hume George later wrote of her mentor Leslie Fiedler, that she "could
not achieve the act of identification"[26] she needed as a writer; rather,
Ross believed fervently in her "will to win"[27] and was an "Enabling
presence"[28] for Wiseman. It was Ross who urged Wiseman to apply
for a Guggenheim Fellowship and suggested potential referees. The
success of her application was due in large part to Ross's foresight and
support, and to the recommendations provided by eminent referees
such as Saul Bellow, David Daiches, Irving Howe, and Meyer Levin.

In 1950, Ross accepted a position in the Department of English
at Queen's University and left Winnipeg for Kingston. Wiseman

Back row (L to R):
unidentified woman,
Margaret Stobie,
unidentified woman

Front row (L to R):
William Stobie,
Adele Wiseman,
Morris Wiseman,
7 October 1949.
Wiseman's home,
490 Burrows Avenue,
Winnipeg.

(Archives and Special
Collections, University of
Manitoba Library)

maintained her tie with the University of Manitoba through Margaret
and William Stobie, professors of English who continued the work of
mentorship begun by Ross. The Stobies took a particular interest in
The Sacrifice and Wiseman was aided by their critical commentary on
her manuscript. In November 1955, Margaret Stobie proved instrumental in publicizing the novel on CBC Radio. Although Wiseman
later cooled her connection with the Stobies—she felt they were too
close to her first novel—their timely and conscientious support helped
launch Wiseman's career. In fact, Malcolm Ross and Margaret and
William Stobie were guiding mentors during Wiseman's long literary
apprenticeship. Each believed in Wiseman's talent, sought in various
ways to foster her ability as a writer, and frequently provided practical
assistance.

At the University of Manitoba, Ross's students included writers
such as Patricia Blondal, Margaret Laurence, Jack Ludwig, and
Adele Wiseman. Ross attested to "a strain of brilliance in the[ir]
blood. . . . They were all excited about their studies—they were
thirsty for ideas. We would meet after class and talk and argue into

the night. I have never known anything like it—before or since."[29] Later, Wiseman remembered Ross as

> the rigorously honest and extraordinarily sensitive critic to whom I submitted my earliest writing. I know I express the gratitude and love of all the generations of students who have been lucky enough to be able to call him their teacher, though not unnaturally I feel that my own generation owes him a particular debt.

> . . . [Malcolm Ross] had the rare ability to communicate intellectual passion, had the effect of awakening the faculties. . . . We shared the excitement of learning a way of learning, an attitude to experience, to standards, and to larger goals. We became comrades, grew in self-confidence and determination to enter and help create and extend the cultural life of this country. Malcolm Ross taught us to look to literature not simply as a by-product but as a prime value, as the expression of the quality of a society, as witness to the soul of a culture.[30]

Ross delighted in Wiseman, who enlivened his seminars with her sharp mind and love of debate.[31] Most of the discussions they shared, however, took place outside class, in his office, where she would bring her stories for Ross to read and evaluate. One in particular stunned him. "Squeezed too thin,"[32] the narrative begged to be developed into a novel. Ross's encouragement, along with the counsel of Margaret and William Stobie, later brought that story to fruition as *The Sacrifice*, its central event a parodic ritual slaughter of Laiah by Abraham.

The Sacrifice incorporates the story of "an actual murder in Manitoba" when Wiseman was sixteen: "An old Jewish man killed a woman he had been courting. She had been kind of leading him on. That summer I had been working at a fruit stall in the market, and the old man who owned the stall used to sit outside with his cronies and discuss this terrible shameful case."[33] This incident later galvanized Wiseman's writing. As she thought her "way back to that particular story of the murder,"[34] her focus shifted from two boys who were at the centre of her short story—they developed as Moses and Aaron—to the old Jew as her protagonist, Abraham.

Wiseman took advantage of every scholarly and literary opportunity available to her at the University of Manitoba. In fact, upon graduation in 1949 (with an Honours BA, English major, and psychology minor), so certain was she of her vocation that she applied to the renowned Graduate College of the State University of Iowa for advanced study in creative writing (now known as the University of Iowa's Writer's Workshop). When her acceptance arrived—affording a considerable chance to work with esteemed writing faculty—she had to make a choice either to continue her studies or to take the time she needed to develop her short story into a novel. Courageously, she chose the latter and, after working one "year to save for a one-way ticket,"[35] determined to leave for London, England, where her friend Margaret Laurence had secured her a job.

In London, Wiseman cemented her growing friendship with Laurence. Although each had attended the University of Manitoba, they first encountered one another at the Ukrainian Labour Temple in Winnipeg's North End, where each was seeking newspaper work. At the time of their marriage in 1947, however, Margaret and her husband Jack Laurence, "[b]y some fluke" as Wiseman tells it,[36] moved into a flat opposite Wiseman's home at 490 Burrows Avenue and their relationship, founded on a mutual sense of vocation, developed quickly and endured until Laurence's death in January 1987. In fact, political connections had led the Laurences to the Burrows Avenue flat, located in the home of Bill Ross (no relation to Malcolm), who later headed Manitoba's Communist Party.

As peers and aspiring writers, Wiseman and Laurence could not offer one another "the experience of experience."[37] They could, however, support one another through friendship and validate their common desire to become published writers; to serve, in fact, as one another's mentor, if a mentor is—as Deborah Digges describes—"one who recognizes you among the millions, calls you forward to bear witness to what you have seen and heard and felt."[38] The nurturing friendship between Wiseman and Laurence continued throughout their adult lives and often was maintained across vast distances. In *The Diviners*, Laurence paid special tribute to their alliance when she modelled a fictional character, Morag Gunn's good friend Ella Gerson, after Adele Wiseman.

Laurence wrote to Wiseman on 21 July 1963: "Your letters make me feel I actually exist."[39] Almost two years later, on 23 February 1965, Wiseman wrote to her friend: "Please write, to me and at your work. There are few other satisfactions."[40] Implicit in these brief comments is the premise that neither the individual nor her writing fully existed without endorsement by the other. In fact, Wiseman and Laurence, largely through a correspondence of many years, formed a literary partnership that insulated them from the elite of Canadian modernism, defined by Carole Gerson as "a loose 'invisible college' distinctly masculine in gender and taste that determined who and what got into print and into anthologies, and which works received prizes and plaudits."[41] What Wiseman and Laurence learned over time was evident early in their letters: that female friendship could help sustain their vocational commitment to writing.

The correspondence between Wiseman and Laurence, housed at York University's Clara Thomas Archives, spans a friendship of more than four decades. A total of more than 300 letters in the Adele

Wiseman fonds and the Margaret Laurence fonds attests to a lasting alliance that came to a close with Laurence's death on 4 January 1987. The correspondence is a testimonial to two women committed equally to their professional and personal engagements, not the least of which was their friendship. Their letters created a women's world that privileged what writer Gail Scott has called "the undernurtured woman's voice, badly heard outside in . . . a 'man's world'"[42] of publishing practice and literary reception.

Today, when these women's works are read in the context of widespread assumptions about distinctive female traditions and cultures, the letters between Wiseman and Laurence remind us of the extent to which they lived within—if not always in agreement with—the parameters of a solidly patriarchal world. Wiseman's powerful first novel is rooted in the conflicts among three generations of men in an immigrant Jewish family. Laurence's first works and many of her short stories focussed on male figures in a male-dominated culture and were submitted for approval to Jack Laurence, whom his wife regarded for years as her best critic. The 1940s, 1950s, and much of the 1960s were dominated by male writers. Wiseman was aware of the work of contemporary American writers such as Saul Bellow, Norman Mailer, and William Styron, and Laurence had a lifelong admiration for the fiction of Joyce Cary. Editors and publishers were men, and so were agents. For Wiseman, it was Kildare Dobbs who accepted *The Sacrifice* at Macmillan in Toronto and then sent it to Marshall Ayres Best at Viking Press in New York. She successfully approached Victor Gollancz in London about British publication. For Laurence, her first publishers were Lovat Dickson and Alan Maclean at Macmillan in London, then Jack McClelland in Toronto and Alfred Knopf in New York. For a brief while, Wiseman and Laurence used New York literary agent Willis Kingsley Wing.

Wiseman and Laurence apprehended themselves as outsiders, peripheral to modernist Canadian culture. Theirs was a hazardous venture that involved economic risks and personal sacrifices, some of which they could anticipate, others that presented themselves with little notice. Writers rarely know financial security, for example, and the demanding, solitary nature of their work often melds uneasily with family life. Wiseman and Laurence understood the key role each played in the other's life—they viewed themselves as allies and mentors—which gave them strength to confront professional and personal challenges. Moreover, as their career paths diverged, neither woman exploited her shifting position of power. They shared a common goal, undertaken with apprehension and caution, to write from their perspectives as women and to stake out a territory within prevailing literary culture, thereby breaking ground for themselves and contemporary Canadian female writers.

Over forty years, Wiseman and Laurence exchanged letters about their personal lives, their writing, and the difficulties of the writing life. Many of these letters were written during Laurence's extended stay in Africa between 1950 and 1957, years of literary apprenticeship for both women, when Laurence and her family moved frequently. This led to efforts to lighten her household possessions and an unfortunate decision to dispose of Wiseman's letters written from London, Rome, and Winnipeg, where she lived and worked during the 1950s.[43] This was a period of intense activity for Wiseman that included the composition and publication of *The Sacrifice*. In fact, in a correspondence that begins in the late 1940s, Wiseman's letters date only from 1962, rather late in an otherwise remarkable record of two unusual women.

Laurence could have committed the rash act of discarding Wiseman's letters only because she had yet to recognize their literary significance and historical value. In fact, it was not until the 1960s, when she was enjoying the successful publication of three of her Manawaka novels and had come to regard herself as a professional, that Laurence began in earnest to safeguard her letters with a view to their potential importance to literary scholarship. In contrast to Laurence, Wiseman understood early on that her literary correspondence would have far-reaching significance. Although she did not keep copies of her own letters, she assiduously saved those she received from Laurence. Moreover, since Wiseman wrote less frequently than Laurence, there was a natural imbalance in the number of letters penned by each woman. The result is a correspondence in which one writer's voice predominates over the other.

In the first extant letter in the correspondence, dated Blue Monday and addressed to Wiseman and her family in Winnipeg while Laurence was visiting her home town of Neepawa, Manitoba, Laurence exclaimed: "I am writing to you because if I don't I shall explode (mentally that is.) . . . I'm sorry if this epistle appears a trifle disjointed, but my need is great, believe me."[44] By fall 1947, the likely date of the letter, Wiseman and Laurence already had formed a connection that would sustain them during trying times. While she enjoyed the intimacy of her marriage to Jack Laurence, which had taken place on 13 September 1947, Laurence continued to seek shelter in her nurturing friendship with Wiseman and her family. The urgent tone of Laurence's appeal to Wiseman characterized many of the subsequent letters exchanged by the two women, whose need for one another's personal and professional reassurance increased rather than diminished over the years.

During the fifties the writers were separated by vast distances. They met briefly in London in August 1950 when Wiseman arrived for the first of two extended residencies in Britain and Laurence was preparing to leave for Africa, where her husband had accepted an engineering post. While living in London, Laurence had secured a job for her friend at the Stepney Jewish Girls' (B'nai B'rith) Club and Settlement in London's East End, one of many favours—often carried out at opposite ends of the globe—that became reciprocal over the years. On 19 July 1950, Laurence could write from London to her good friend in Winnipeg: "Well, kid, your troubles are over . . . for a while, anyway! I went to see Miss Gerson at the Stepney Jewish Girls Club, and had a long talk with her about you."[45] At Laurence's suggestion, Wiseman had written to Jewish social work agencies in the hope of securing employment that would facilitate her move to London. Having written to Phyllis Gerson, warden of Stepney, Wiseman had asked Laurence to meet with Gerson on her behalf. Laurence reported back: "[Y]ou can begin work on a part-time basis, in exchange for your room and board and some pocket-money . . . helping the group leaders with the junior club activities."[46] Wiseman had worked as playground supervisor for the Winnipeg Public Parks Board, so she felt suited to the job and readily agreed to the arrangement, especially since Laurence assured her that Gerson knew her main "object in coming to England"[47] was to make time to write. Wiseman accepted Gerson's offer of part-time employment and accommodation and made preparations to leave for London.

Phyllis Gerson, an English social worker and graduate of the London School of Economics, was a remarkable woman. She had been a leader of Stepney from 1929 to 1944, had spent two years with the First Jewish Relief Unit, and then had returned to Stepney as its warden, a position she held until her retirement in 1973. She was also a Justice of the Peace in Hackney Juvenile Court and had been made a Member of the Order of the British Empire.

In London, Wiseman was fortunate to work under Phyllis Gerson. Gerson provided room and board in exchange for Wiseman's work at Stepney, but she always knew Wiseman to be a writer. In ways both practical and emotional, Gerson facilitated Wiseman's writing. She ensured that Wiseman had ample opportunity to concentrate on her work and regularly offered her own flat as a place of refuge where the aspiring author could spend uninterrupted time on her first novel. She also served as mentor to the young writer, who recognized in Gerson a deep vocational commitment. Gerson inspired with her creative energy and her willingness to embrace people from diverse backgrounds, qualities that Wiseman admired in her own mother. In fact, Gerson offered a nurturing attention that resembled the care of a mother: she proffered food and shelter, attended to Wiseman during times of illness, and intuited her emotional needs. Stepney was Wiseman's base in London and, following her departure for Rome in 1951, she began a correspondence with Gerson that lasted until the latter's death in 1990. Throughout a lifetime of letter writing, the women extended the connection they formed in London into an exchange of intimate details of their daily lives.

Over the years, Wiseman had numerous opportunities to repay Laurence for having contacted Gerson on her behalf. When she lived in Montreal during the sixties, for example, she granted *Time* magazine an interview about her friend, whose novel *The Fire-Dwellers* had recently been published. On 25 March 1969, Wiseman issued Laurence a warning:

> I can just imagine what . . . [the article will] be like when they're through selecting & patching & finding clever angles. Fooey. But it'll be publicity. Forgive me in advance. Whatever I did say was well meant. In fact . . . [the reporter] kept trying to get me to tell anecdotes or an anecdote that would make you seem perhaps a little less perfect, perhaps a little humanly ridiculous. The only ones I could think of made me the Charley, which I usually am.[48]

Pregnancy, childbirth, and especially the rearing of children were favourite subjects throughout the correspondence. In their letters,

Wiseman and Laurence felt free to discuss issues that were important to them both as women and as writers. At a time when they often felt excluded from the patriarchal culture of authorship and when, as poet Adrienne Rich explains, "to a lesser or greater extent, every woman writer . . . [wrote] for men even when . . . she was supposed to be addressing women,"[49] Wiseman and Laurence communicated frankly and without constraint within the privacy of their letters. As Rich argues, "Everywhere, women working in the common world of men are denied that integrity of work and life which can only be found in an emotional and intellectual connectedness with ourselves and other women."[50] For Wiseman and Laurence, work and life came together in their correspondence.

Wiseman, in particular, was open about the impact of pregnancy on her daily life, a facet of women's lives that only recently has been explored in literature. As novelist Carol Shields once noted with characteristic irony, "conception, birth, and motherhood have been effectively locked out of literature from its beginnings. The transcendence of these human experiences and their centrality in the human drama have been deemed too banal, too boring, too cute, too messy for high art."[51] For Wiseman, who became pregnant at the late age of forty, the opportunity to share her experience with Laurence was liberating.

Wiseman's letter to Laurence of 28 December 1968 was a mixture of elation and anxiety:

> I've never quite felt so out-of-myself, possessed, usurped, before. My whole mechanism seems to have gone wonky. Food, hitherto my solace & sustenance, has turned prime enemy, & I have to overcome revulsion in order to eat, which I do periodically, nevertheless, for fear of starving the guest. But ugh, the odor! Anyway, it is kind of funny, at my age, & a part of me is enjoying the long delayed,

primal experience, when it can believe it. . . . I begin to understand the anxieties of prenatal women. Just let it be normal, is all I ask.[52]

Since Laurence's children were born in the fifties, she was the experienced elder, well qualified to listen and advise her friend, who was charting new territory:

Sleep on, sleep on in majesty! Don't feel guilty about wanting to sleep. Golly, when I was pregnant with both kids I nearly hibernated for 9 months—I simply could not get enough sleep. . . . All one can say, really, is—hang on, things will get better. . . . as kids do (thank god) get older and one is increasingly less responsible for them. Personally, I am delighted that my kids are becoming more and more responsible for themselves—I am not at all tempted to hang onto them; the decrease in my responsibility is like a weight lifted from my mind.[53]

Wiseman's pregnancy brought her closer to Laurence. With the birth of her only child, she entered a world that Laurence knew well. From 1969 onward, their correspondence was replete with talk of children and the joy and agony they brought their mothers. Moreover, their homes always were open to one another; soon after the birth of her daughter Tamara, for example, Wiseman hosted Laurence and her two children, who visited Montreal in August 1969. The two families often visited, and Wiseman and Laurence came to think of themselves as substitute mothers to one another's children. Although their career paths diverged over the years, their children were another common ground that brought them together and through whom their intense bond of friendship continually was reforged.

Wiseman was the one to whom Laurence fairly screamed across the Atlantic when she received good news. On 1 December 1959 she was able to proclaim:

> Macmillan in England has accepted it [i.e. *This Side Jordan*]!
>
> > Hurrah!
> > > Hurrah!
> > > > HURRAH!
> > [They want 10,000 words deleted. A mere bagatelle! And it *is* too long—they're right.]
>
> Love from your erstwhile pessimistic but now fantastically optimistic friend—JML[54]

Later, writing of *The Stone Angel* in a letter conspicuously dated Valentine's Day, 14 February 1963, Laurence announced:

> ALAN MACLEAN (MACMILLAN'S) LIKES *HAGAR* [the novel's orig-inal title]! HE LIKES IT! CAN IT BE TRUE? He has just phoned, and I am in something like a state of shock. . . . Adele, I feel as though my faith in life, in myself, in everything, has been miraculously restored to me. . . . [M]y uncertainties about myself were so marked and of such long standing that I cannot help feeling an enormous relief to hear that Alan likes the book. . . .[55]

Throughout their long friendship, Laurence's need to share the thrill of success with Wiseman never waned. She knew that only Wiseman could appreciate fully the enormous effort and sacrifice that each of her novels demanded, and how bittersweet each success was in light of that effort. Moreover, her friend understood the true extent of Laurence's achievement as a woman working within a profession dominated by men. To judge by her extant letters to Laurence, Wiseman likely wrote of her own early triumphs with a similar exuberance.

In addition to rejoicing in one another's professional accomplishments, Wiseman and Laurence passed support, encouragement, and advice back and forth in their letters. As ambitious young women, they jointly vowed—only partly in jest—to win the Governor General's Award for fiction. Later, when Wiseman was having difficulty placing her play, *The Lovebound*, Laurence urged: "DON'T GIVE UP ON THE PLAY!!!!!!!"[56] When she heard that *Crackpot*, Wiseman's second novel, had been rejected, Laurence's response on 3 September 1968 was equally blunt and emphatic—"Viking are out of their minds"[57]—and she later contacted publisher Jack McClelland on behalf of her disappointed friend, thereby facilitating publication of the novel.

The most compelling evidence, however, of the friendship shared by Wiseman and Laurence are the intimate passages of comfort that marked their extraordinary correspondence. In September 1968, when a frustrated Wiseman was attempting to place *Crackpot* with a publisher, Laurence wrote the following moving passage to her friend:

> I have...always felt...[that]...your writing...works on many different levels; that it has a quality of interwovedness...; that people appear and inhabit the reader's mind not only as themselves but also as archetypes; that the echoes are not the ones made from yodelling at a mountain but rather the voices heard in the caves, the things about ourselves that we would frequently rather not know, or the things about ourselves and others which we perceive only dimly and from time to time, here made real and undeniable. You see, I don't believe and never have believed

that you were writing for any one generation, Adele. . . . I knew . . . [early on] that you had committed yourself to the god more than I could—more than it was given to me to do, because really it has nothing to do with what one wants, one way or another.[58]

To this characteristically open statement, Wiseman responded in kind: "Thanks for your letters. I appreciate them, need I say how much? . . . I know you are paying me an enormous compliment, but at the same time you are unfairly denigrating yourself, as you've always done."[59]

As Adrienne Rich explains, "It is not generosity that makes women in community support and nourish each other. It is rather what Whitman called the 'hunger for equals'—the desire for a context in which our own strivings will be amplified, quickened, lucidified, through those of our peers."[60] Wiseman and Laurence trusted and nurtured one another as peers. They were blessed by a friendship that provided, in addition to emotional support and intellectual stimulation, a sheltering sense of sisterhood.

By January 1987, the month of Laurence's death, Wiseman's community of women writers had widened considerably and had become a source of great comfort.[61] The American writer Tillie Olsen, for example, insisted she had an incomparable friend in Wiseman. Nonetheless, Wiseman felt the loss of Laurence keenly, as Malcolm Ross understood: "No one will miss Margaret as much as you [Adele]. . . . It is a terrible loss and I know how deeply you mourn. The two of you are interlocked in memories of mine that go back to the 'forties in Winnipeg. Be sure that I share your grief."[62] Although she was "fortunate enough to have [Margaret's life] embedded in mine," seven years after Laurence's death, Wiseman still was unable to fully "assimilate"[63] the loss. She continued to mourn her friend, whose death she believed "was received by Canadians much as the deaths of presidents are received in the United States."[64] In recognition of their friendship, Wiseman was invited by Trent University, where Laurence had been chancellor between 1980 and 1983, to deliver the first annual Margaret Laurence Tribute on 10 March 1988. The sustaining relationship between Wiseman and Laurence, formed early and at a time when there were few women writers in Canada, was among the most important of their respective connections. Having come to regard one another as "sister friend,"[65] Wiseman and Laurence modelled other friendships as mentorships, after their own alliance.

IN LONDON, WISEMAN HAD MET MORDECAI RICHLER when they both were aspiring and impecunious writers. In an interview in 1999, he recalled "a gentle, decent, unpretentious person, more involved with the Jewish community than the literary community."[66] Having arrived in London directly from Winnipeg, Wiseman's lack of sophistication as a young writer is not surprising. Moreover, as Richler noted, Wiseman did not move in London literary circles and preferred a quiet life working as Student Club Leader for children ages five to fourteen, editing the *Stepney Jester*, an in-house newsletter, and writing *The Sacrifice*.

We do not know for certain how much Wiseman participated in the cultural life of London during her year there.[67] It is possible, however, to extrapolate from Laurence's side of their correspondence a superficial sense of Wiseman's activities in London, Rome, and Winnipeg, where she lived in the early fifties. Clearly, she was writing. Throughout 1951, Laurence urged: "[I hope] that you're finding some time for your own work";[68] "that your writing is going forward, and that the job's all right, and that you aren't discouraged";[69] "[H]ow is your writing? That is the question";[70] "How is your book? . . . Let me know the details some time. Where have you got with it?"[71] Writing to Wiseman in Rome, Laurence confirmed, "I'm very glad that you're working on your book now . . . how is it coming along? How much have you got done? Where are you with [it?]";[72] and persistently, "Please write soon, and give us all the news about . . . the book";[73] "Is the novel still coming along well?"[74] Laurence also wrote to console her friend, who had been disappointed in love: "[T]ake care of yourself . . . don't try starving or anything, will you? As an economy, I mean. I hope the book will progress again now";[75] "Don't let anything or anyone put you off from continuing . . . [your book], will you?"[76]

Wiseman spent much of 1952 in Italy working for the Overseas School of Rome, first as a grade five teacher and later as vice-superintendent of its summer school camp. More important, however, is the opportunity that summer provided for her writing. In Rome, she lived and wrote as "a free woman" in "the process of becoming a Canadian writer."[77] Through her work at the Overseas School, she learned the language of her campers well enough to read novels and write doggerel in Italian. In the diary she kept while living at Via Catria 1, published in her *Memoirs*, she wrote on 28 June 1952: "I have been writing a lot. Two days ago I killed off Isaac and I'm afraid I still haven't recovered" (60). By 18 July, she noted, "Yesterday I did a lot of writing—ten typed pages. Abraham killed Laiah—it's all still unreal in my mind, but there, it's done. I really don't want to leave him so. I love Abraham after all this time" (61).

These brief excerpts from Wiseman's diary suggest a young writer immersed in her work and moving out of a literary apprenticeship that had begun when, still in grade five, she "made the conscious decision that easy victories were not enough. Someday I was going to write what was hardest and what was most important to me" (13). During her time overseas, Wiseman had few responsibilities and was free to concentrate on her writing. She described "the experience of living in a foreign country, particularly when you're writing fiction, . . . [as]

a luxury . . . because your inner world, your growing fiction, is so clearly separate from the world around you. In a sense the world around you is less real than that thing you're clarifying on paper."[78] By 24 July 1952, Wiseman had completed the first draft of her novel, which she had conceived in two parts. Upon completion, however, she admitted in her diary, "I don't think there will be a Part II" (61). Two days later, on 26 July, she began the second draft, "which means changing a bit, adding a bit etc. I haven't gotten into the big work yet, but am coming to one of my first snags. So much word juggling, but I'm trying to purify. In about two months I sail for home. What next?" (61–62). Wiseman returned to Winnipeg and her parents' home in the fall of 1952, after one year in London and another year in Rome. True to her intention, she returned to Canada with a draft typescript of *The Sacrifice*. In the shadow of the Holocaust that still lay over Europe, Wiseman had completed her narrative of Jewish life in the New World.

DURING THE INTERVENING PERIOD in Winnipeg, until her return to London in 1955 for a further two years, Wiseman held a number of jobs while she revised her novel. She resumed work as tutor and marker for the Department of English at the University of Manitoba. For a time she was technical assistant at Dominion Food Pests Entomological Laboratory, and then executive secretary to the Royal Winnipeg Ballet. Apparently, Wiseman did not feel compromised by such employment. As Laurence explained, "Of course, it will mean that the book doesn't get done as quickly, but as you say, you're far enough with it now that you know you will finish it, and the job[s] will give you the opportunity to save something."[79]

Wiseman's renewed connection with the university's Department of English proved fortuitous. By 10 June 1953, Margaret and William Stobie had read her novel. Once again, Laurence offered invaluable commentary as she intuited the Stobies' key role in the publishing history of *The Sacrifice*: "I'm so glad the Stobies like your book— that is *really good*. Keep on with the good work, whatever you do. Someday, Adele, that is going to be a really fine novel."[80] The Stobies gave Wiseman useful criticism of her work in draft, and by the end of 1953 she felt her novel close enough to completion that Laurence could proclaim: "I really admire the way you've stuck with it, Adele, and I honestly believe it won't be too long before I'm receiving my autographed copy of it!"[81] By 7 April 1954, Wiseman had asked the Stobies to comment on revisions she had made to her novel, a delay that incited the following response from Laurence: "What are you going to do—I mean, to whom are you going to send it? . . . I'm so anxious to read it."[82]

Laurence's belief in imminent publication for *The Sacrifice* was only slightly premature. By 20 June 1955, Margaret Stobie had arranged to read an excerpt from *The Sacrifice* on the CBC Radio program *Anthology*. Stobie would have brought the novel to the attention of Robert Weaver, who created and produced *Anthology* (1954 to 1985) as a showcase for contemporary Canadian writing, and who became a friend of Wiseman.[83] After completing a degree in English and philosophy at the University of Toronto, Weaver had joined the CBC in 1948. Described as "the godfather of Canadian writing,"[84] he was instrumental in nurturing and shaping the careers of many writers, including those of luminaries Alice Munro and Mordecai Richler, for example. George Woodcock claims that, as "a program organizer and producer for radio, Weaver played an important role as a kind of impresario in the Canadian literary world, encouraging writers, producing their works, and giving them employment as critics and commentators."[85] Further, as critic JoAnn McCaig points out, Weaver was a "salaried employee" of the CBC who "had little to gain financially from the success or failure of his proteges."[86] Rather, his drive to support Canadian writers was spurred by his passion for literature and was fuelled by the cultural nationalism of the fifties and sixties.

As early as October 1949, Weaver had asked Wiseman to submit short stories for possible broadcast on the CBC program *Canadian Short Stories* (1946 to 1954). The next year, he reiterated his offer to consider her work. Having read her story "Nor Youth Nor Age," published in the University of Manitoba's *Creative Campus*, Weaver urged: "I'd be very much interested in seeing any material of yours which you feel might prove suitable."[87] In response, Wiseman sent Weaver a copy of "Nor Youth Nor Age" and asked for his comments. Although he was unable to accept the work for broadcast—it included "too many characters" and he found its opening "too impressionistic" for radio listeners—Weaver hoped that Wiseman would submit more fiction "just as soon as you have anything on hand."[88] In May 1950, when Weaver learned that Wiseman was at work on a novel, he wrote encouragingly: "I might also point out to you that on one or two occasions we have used chapters from novels in broadcasts."[89]

Weaver recognized Wiseman's talent and enjoyed her personality. Whenever possible, he offered the opportunity to publicize her work. Throughout the forties and fifties, Weaver solicited material from Wiseman, either for broadcast on CBC Radio or for publication in his literary journal, *Tamarack Review* (1956 to 1982).[90] In 1959, for example, Weaver insisted, "I really want to have a story from you."[91] He hoped to stimulate Wiseman's writing with an offer of the substantial sum of $1000 in payment for a story. The story she produced was too long, however, and, characteristically, Wiseman refused to edit her work. In the late 1950s, when Weaver offered to have her play *The Lovebound* edited by "someone who knows how to write for radio,"[92] Wiseman refused. She would not agree to have her four-hour play edited to a ninety-minute broadcast, as required by the CBC. Although he could not "get to first base" with Wiseman on *The Lovebound*, Weaver

understood that the play "was enormously important to her emotion-
ally"[93] and his genuine interest in Wiseman was clear in his occasional
letters written "because I wanted to . . . for no special reason, I hasten
to say, and certainly not business."[94] Later, following Wiseman's move
in 1969 to the greater Toronto area where Weaver also lived, author
and producer continued their friendship over the telephone and in
person. Wiseman would have shared her friend Margaret Laurence's
regard for Weaver as the writers' advocate: "I think he has done more
good to Canadian writers than the Can. Council. I also like him very
much, partly because I think he is a courageous man."[95]

Weaver recalled in 2000 that, while on a business trip to Montreal
with William French, literary editor of the *Globe and Mail*, he stayed
at a hotel near Wiseman's apartment on Drummond Street. When
she rushed over to greet Weaver, Wiseman became the unknowing
source of an anecdote that French afterwards would relate with relish:
"Anywhere Weaver goes in Canada, a beautiful young woman comes
up and grabs him."[96]

Laurence had an opportunity to read her friend's novel during
an extended Canadian vacation, when she visited the Wisemans in
Winnipeg in May and July 1954, and she responded to its "penetrating
and yet deeply sympathetic analysis of the Jewish community. . . . You
have something . . . without which no writer can ever be great and
maybe not even good, and that quality is love and compassion."[97] By
July 1954, the Stobies had read Wiseman's revised novel and offered
additional suggestions. Although he regarded Margaret Stobie "as a
friendly witness,"[98] Malcolm Ross, who considered *The Sacrifice* "one
of the best first novels I have ever read,"[99] also offered Wiseman sage
counsel: "Too many cooks might spoil the broth. You might be wise
to make whatever changes you feel necessary . . . and then get it off
to a publisher forthwith. Contrary opinions might occur and do little
more than confuse you at this stage—I'd go straight ahead revising just

as much as you think the criticism properly demands."[100] Overcoming her initial objections to the Stobies' comments, Wiseman turned her attention to *The Sacrifice* and soon reported to Laurence that the work "is shaping up ok."[101] Having, as she felt, "compress[ed] too much,"[102] Wiseman struggled to improve the ending of her novel. Despite Margaret Stobie's advice, however, she would not alter the climactic scene of murder. Later, Wiseman distanced herself from the Stobies. Robert Weaver explained in 2000, "Too many people knew about Margaret Stobie's involvement with *The Sacrifice* and Adele really wanted to think of it as *her* book, not as a collaborative effort."[103] In all likelihood, however, the Stobies' assistance was intended to help a novice writer refine and sharpen a highly original work of fiction.

In July 1955, Malcolm Ross invited an "obviously ambitious" Wiseman[104] to attend an important conference held at Queen's University. The theme, "The Writer, His Media, and the Public," attracted an eclectic group of writers, publishers, broadcasters, and academics.[105] The complex series of events that resulted in publication of her first novel were set in motion at that conference. As Ross tells it, Wiseman arrived in Kingston a day before publisher Jack McClelland. The connection between publisher and professor dated back to summer 1946, when returned veteran Jack McClelland was completing his undergraduate degree at the University of Toronto and enrolled in a course taught by Ross. In July 1954, when Wiseman first met McClelland to discuss "a job in the publishing business," the publisher had asked for "the chance to look at"[106] her completed novel. Ross now counted on showing McClelland the typescript of *The Sacrifice* in the hope that McClelland and Stewart might publish the work.

By next morning, however, Kildare Dobbs, who was present at the conference in his capacity as editor with Macmillan of Canada, had been introduced to Wiseman by Weaver. Weaver's high praise

Kildare Dobbs, c1970.

(Archives and Special Collections, University of Manitoba Library)

for Wiseman's novel so affected Dobbs that he felt impelled to act instantly and, after skimming the typescript, he offered to publish *The Sacrifice*.[107] The switch occurred swiftly, "more or less by accident,"[108] and Ross, who felt he could not blame a young, inexperienced author for accepting Dobbs's offer, always "mourned that incident"[109] as a significant loss. Ross may have thought that by accepting Macmillan's offer, Wiseman had lost a potential advocate in Jack McClelland. In fact, McClelland proved to be an important ally when, nearly two decades later, he offered to publish her second novel. Dobbs believed that he was "the first person in publishing to recognize" Wiseman's talent; in 1999 he admitted to having acted expeditiously on behalf of Macmillan.[110]

Upon return to his office in Toronto, Dobbs took up *The Sacrifice* as his project. He wrote to Macmillan in London to ask if the press would be interested in publishing the novel in Britain. He also prepared a thorough reader's report that impressed Marshall Ayres Best of Viking Press as "one of the best reports I ever saw in my life."[111] Today, Dobbs's earliest response to the novel retains its power:

> Here is a big, solid, serious novel which seems to me superbly done and profoundly moving.

> . . . Its richness and complexity defy reduction to a mere summary of outstanding events. If it is slow in starting it is all firmly realised and the characterization is flawless. Nothing is contrived, nothing evaded, but its seriousness doesn't at all preclude humour and (in a good deal of it) there is a masterly restrained irony.

> . . . I believe that in Miss Wiseman, who is 27, we have a novelist of unusual power. I don't say she is promising, because I believe this novel represents something better than that—an achieved success.

> To make it a commercial success is another question. I cannot believe that a U.S. publisher will not be found for the book, but in any case we owe it to ourselves and to Canadian literature to publish it.[112]

Moved by her "humanity and breadth of vision," Dobbs was convinced of Wiseman's talent and his affection for *The Sacrifice* soon transferred to its author.[113] Engaged by Wiseman's charm, warmth, and humour, he worked on her behalf throughout his years as editor at Macmillan.

THAT JULY OF 1955, at the Queen's University conference where the fate of her first novel was sealed, Wiseman had arrived in Kingston too late to enter the room she had reserved in the university's residence. She searched for an unlocked car and there she spent her first night in Kingston. At their initial meeting, Wiseman conveyed this story of spirit, nerve, and determination to Dobbs. Soon, it became a private joke between writer and editor. When Wiseman was living in London during negotiations over *The Sacrifice*, Dobbs wrote: "I hope you are having a good time . . . and that if you do have to spend the night in a car, you will choose at least a Rolls Bentley."[114]

The urbane, cosmopolitan, and well-travelled Dobbs was born in India, educated in Ireland and Cambridge, and had served in the Royal Navy during the Second World War.[115] In 1952, when he immigrated to Canada, Dobbs joined Macmillan as editor. Throughout his ten-year association with the firm, Dobbs maintained a connection with Wiseman.

Having brought Wiseman to the attention of Macmillan, Dobbs was her initial contact at the publishing house. Affably, he wrote to her in Montreal prior to her departure for London, where she lived and worked at the Stepney Jewish Girls' Club while she revised *The Sacrifice*:

> [T]his is a valediction forbidding mourning. I hope you have a good sea voyage and that you will write and tell us all about it, when you reach England. Wave a hand for me at the Irish coast as you go by. And when you are sitting in the Nag's Head or the Antelope or some such place—having a gin and limey—drink to your friends in Toronto of the churches.[116]

Dobbs's experience of Britain coloured his letters to Wiseman, in which he urged often: "[D]on't stay too long with the limeys and come back to us soon. In the opinion of my well travelled self, right here in Toronto is the most exciting place there is";[117] and if "London is the true seat of culture! Well, then, down with culture."[118]

As a Canadian firm with a limited market, Macmillan regularly sought an American co-publisher for its books. American publication, with its large market potential, lessened the financial risk associated with Canadian publication. John Morgan Gray, president of the Macmillan Company of Canada, described the practice of sending a "manuscript to a publisher in the States or Britain, or . . . the book to a literary agent who will act for the author. This kind of helpful activity has often been . . . interpreted as meaning that the Canadian publisher 'won't take a chance' unless somebody makes up his mind for him; but with many books it is the way he can serve the author best."[119] The simultaneous publication of American and Canadian editions of the same work was general practice at mid-century. In fact, Viking Press prepared the Canadian edition of *The Sacrifice* for Macmillan.

Throughout negotiations with Viking, Dobbs's regular telegrams kept Wiseman abreast of developments and his letters were reassuring: "Above all, don't worry. Good novels like yours just don't go unpublished."[120] After some delay on Viking's part, which frustrated Dobbs, who believed firmly in the quality of Wiseman's work, he could take pleasure in delivering good news. On 20 October 1955, he wrote: "[M]y own spirits had been rather damped by the delay in hearing from Viking. I had expected they would break all precedent and call us long distance to ask 'Who *is* this girl? Why haven't we heard of her before?' As a matter of fact, that is precisely what they did yesterday."[121] The earliest letters between Dobbs and Wiseman consolidated a connection between editor and author and convinced Wiseman that Macmillan would act with integrity to protect their mutual interests. Dobbs's commitment to Wiseman, both professional and personal, shaped her lasting relationship with Macmillan.

Their correspondence charted Wiseman's novel's progress toward publication. In a letter of 20 July 1956, Dobbs congratulated Wiseman on having arranged British publication of *The Sacrifice* by Victor Gollancz: "I hope you'll have a roaring success on both sides of the Atlantic."[122] Following a Macmillan sales conference, at which she was praised "antiphonally," Dobbs wrote playfully:

> Versicle: Blessed be Adele Wiseman.
> Antiphon: Who hath written a splendid book.
> Versicle: At three dollars and ninety-five cents.
> Antiphon: This is a lot of book for your money.[123]

Dobbs's dynamic personality—fired, no doubt, by the apparent success of *The Sacrifice*—imbued his later correspondence. He hoped, for example, that Wiseman would give herself time, following the triumph of her novel, "to lie about on ormolu couches smoking jewelled cigars and drinking pink champagne."[124] When he learned that *The Sacrifice* had won the Governor General's Award for fiction in 1956, Dobbs sent Wiseman a gracious "note to say that I think the judges who chose your novel . . . do not so much honour you as themselves and all of us."[125] When her book received the Beta Sigma Phi Award, Dobbs paid Wiseman his deepest compliment: "I am, personally, very pleased at all this public accolade for you. But my own greatest pleasure came long ago, when I first read that beautiful, momentous book; and left it and, like Moses, looked about me at my fellow men. I bless you for it. How should I congratulate you?"[126] Dobbs maintained his high opinion of *The Sacrifice*. In an interview in 1999, he recalled "a very promising, very achieved first novel. Adele knows what she's doing in *The Sacrifice*."[127]

By December 1956, at the suggestion of her former professor and mentor Malcolm Ross, Wiseman had begun the process of applying for a Guggenheim Fellowship and Dobbs soon was "busy swearing that you are Sophocles, Moses, Dante and all rolled into one: we do this that you may be supported by the Guggenheim foundation."[128] Nonetheless, he took the opportunity to note that Wiseman's proposed project, her play *The Lovebound*, although ambitious, seemed "inartistic."[129]

In fact, as early as September 1956, prior to publication of *The Sacrifice*, Dobbs's letters implied concern over Wiseman's continuing work. His early joke, "Before you get cracking (unless you have started already) on your second masterpiece (mistresspiece for a lady novelist?),"[130] resonated across subsequent letters to Wiseman. When she wrote to reassure him of her ability and determination to complete a largely unformulated project, Dobbs was delighted to hear "that you are at work again."[131] On 15 September 1958, he noted, "I have often wondered how the work was going," but concluded in his usual friendly way: "The Canadian Literary world is much as it was: darkened by your absence. [Wiseman still was residing in London.] . . . Please be assured of our continued interest and affection!"[132]

In 1999, Dobbs claimed that he and Wiseman were "friends, not very attentive friends, but there was affection between us."[133] Following his departure from Macmillan in 1962, Dobbs and Wiseman maintained their friendship from a distance. If in later years Dobbs became an inattentive friend to Wiseman, he had been the most attentive of editors during his tenure at Macmillan. In letters to Dobbs, Wiseman conveyed appreciation for his work on behalf of *The Sacrifice*. The warmth and natural humour of her correspondence suggest she was comfortable in their relationship. That they maintained a friendship is confirmed, moreover, by Dobbs's visit with Wiseman in the early sixties when, as a Guggenheim Fellow, she lived in New York City. Wiseman's good fortune was to have an editor early in her career who embraced her vision, admired her talent—"there was no tinkering with *The Sacrifice*"[134]—and sought to make her work available to a wide readership.

IN 1946, JOHN MORGAN GRAY was appointed general manager of Macmillan, and in 1955 he became president of the company. Born in Cornwall, Ontario, in 1907, Gray was educated in England—where his father served in the Canadian army during the First World War—and in Canada at Lakefield College, Upper Canada College, and the University of Toronto. Later, he was assistant master at Lakefield College for one year. Prior to serving overseas from 1941 to 1946 in the Intelligence Corps of the First Canadian Army, Gray worked for Macmillan for ten years as educational representative under president Hugh Eayrs, who introduced him to the "endlessly fascinating . . . world of books and writers."[135]

After the Second World War, Gray returned to publishing and the chance to head Macmillan at a time of new growth. Lovat Dickson, one-time director of the Macmillan Company in Britain, explains:

> This was a propitious time to take charge of a Canadian publishing company. The long servitude of the industry to its British and American overlords, which had made many publishers no more than importing agencies, was about to be transformed. Given full power and resources, limited only by British Exchange Control restrictions, Gray was provided with an opportunity to become not only a leader but . . . a spokesman for the trade.[136]

In spite of Dickson's claim, resources remained limited—out of financial necessity, publishers continued as agents for British and American houses—but Canadian publishers did prosper in the post-war years, as they had earlier in the century. The years 1945 and 1946 saw an impressive rise in production of indigenous titles,[137] and a maturing nationalism fed a growing awareness of, and desire for, Canadian art and culture. The CBC and Radio-Canada, which developed during the 1940s and 1950s, for example, featured writing by Canadians. Program organizer Robert Weaver joined the CBC in 1948 and began immediately to solicit work by Canadians, which aired regularly on programs such as *Canadian Short Stories* (1946 to 1954), CBC *Wednesday Night* (1947 to 1963), *Critically Speaking* (1948 to 1967), *Anthology* (1954 to 1985), and *Stories with John Drainie* (1959 to 1965).[138]

John Gray and Kildare Dobbs were preoccupied with arranging American publication of *The Sacrifice* when they finally received word that Macmillan of London was not prepared to issue the novel in Britain. They were communicating with Marshall Ayres Best in New York. Best was open to writing by Canadians. In a later interview, conducted in 1976, he admonished the interviewer for his dismissal of Canadian writing: "We often fail to recognize that they [i.e. Canadians] have their own qualities. Just as we [i.e. Americans] were provincial originally, and became more independent, they have become much more independent; but we haven't really caught up to the fact."[139] Best's Viking Press reader, however, had reported negatively on Wiseman's novel. Gray had written to Best, asking him "to give some priority to the reading of this manuscript," which has "excited us more than any . . . we have seen for several years,"[140] and praising Wiseman's originality and vision: "[I] can't think of anyone likely to do this kind of thing half so well."[141] Then, Viking's final reader's report also lauded the work: "it is as exotic as if it were set on another continent. In a deeper sense, however, it is as universal in its emotions as the Bible."[142] Finally, after reading *The Sacrifice* himself and suggesting minor revisions, on 27 October 1955 Best offered to publish the novel. Having confirmed American publication, Macmillan could proceed with Canadian publication.

Best's reading of Wiseman's novel corroborated Gray's high opinion of the work as mature and accomplished. On 15 November 1955, Best wrote to Wiseman: "I enjoyed my second reading of the manuscript . . . fully as much as the first. Abraham and Moishe and Ruth and Chaim, even Laiah, are now a part of my life. . . . You have written a beautiful and moving book. It seems almost a miracle to me that so mature, so knowing, and skillful a work could be a first novel."[143]

In 1999, Dobbs recalled the real fondness that he, John Gray, and Marshall Best felt for Wiseman. A playful postcard written jointly by Best and Wiseman to Gray when they met in August 1956 in Chartres reveals their open friendship. Best wrote: "The first meeting with this new author was bound to be fun, but in the atmosphere of Chartres it's even more special." Wiseman's brief note expressed her own delight in meeting Best.[144] Wiseman enjoyed a friendly relationship with Best who, like Dobbs and Gray in Canada, worked on her behalf in the United States.

On 8 November 1955, following acceptance of the novel in Toronto and New York, Margaret Stobie read an excerpt of *The Sacrifice* on CBC Radio (for which Wiseman received a fee of ninety dollars) and the buzz surrounding the novel began to escalate. Hoping to pique interest in *The Sacrifice* overseas, John Gray wrote to Juliet Piggott of the Curtis Brown Agency in London: "[Wiseman] might be wise to have an agent for Britain and the Continent and . . . she couldn't do better than talk to you."[145]

In Great Britain, however, Wiseman did not require the services of a literary agent. At the suggestion of her friend Hallam Tennyson, great-grandson of Alfred, Lord Tennyson, she approached the London publisher Victor Gollancz about issuing her novel in Britain. On 22 March 1956, Gollancz offered to publish *The Sacrifice*—"a remarkable and moving achievement"[146]—and advanced Wiseman a royalty payment of £150. In addition, she received a royalty advance of $1000US from Viking and $300Cdn from Macmillan.[147] Unfortunately, little record remains of the relationship between Gollancz and Wiseman. The extant correspondence attests to her congenial, professional connection with VG, as he was known, whose personality has been described as "bold, adventurous, creative and energetic."[148] Certainly, *The Sacrifice* would have appealed to Gollancz's avowed interest in matters Jewish (Gollancz was himself a Jew).[149] That the novel, moreover, already had been accepted for publication by prominent American and Canadian firms may have helped convince Gollancz of its viability in Great Britain.

Having returned to London in October 1955, Wiseman resumed her work at the Stepney Jewish Girls' Club while revising her novel and editing one issue of the *Stepney Jester*. On 10 February 1956, she sent a revised typescript to Viking. It took several months, but on 13 September 1956, *The Sacrifice* was published simultaneously in New York and Toronto; London publication followed on 22 October. The book was priced at $3.95 across North America.

Five thousand copies of the American edition were printed. The Canadian edition consisted of 2500 copies, of which 1038 copies were sold prior to publication. In 1956, Dobbs claimed that *The Sacrifice* had the largest pre-publication sale of a first novel ever published in Canada. When they depleted their stock by 19 October 1956, Viking and Macmillan soon required second impressions of the novel. The second Canadian impression consisted of 1500 copies.[150]

UPON PUBLICATION OF *THE SACRIFICE*, Wiseman was embraced by the media. As Robert Weaver has pointed out, *The Sacrifice* "had a lot of success for a book published by an obscure Winnipeg writer and that was pretty heady."[151] But the success was well earned by a young author who had devoted seven laborious years to writing and revising

Adele Wiseman, c1961.
Photographer: Amy Zahl.
(Macmillan Company of
Canada fonds, McMaster
University Library)

her first novel. Although Wiseman felt publication was anti-climactic, the quality of her effort was noted by reviewers in Canada, the United States, and Great Britain, who, with few exceptions, lauded *The Sacrifice* for its fine execution, its profound characterization of Abraham, and its biblical themes, and thus echoed Kildare Dobbs's earlier response to the work.

M.M. Mitchell of the *Globe and Mail* shared the "suffering and despair" of all "Avroms" and praised the novel's "Biblical atmosphere."[152] In a review entitled "The Abraham Story," James Scott of the Toronto *Telegram* admired Wiseman's "profound sympathy for humanity and a capacity to delineate emotions in . . . the day to day existence of her Abraham."[153] In the Montreal *Gazette*, Lawrence Sabbath read promise in Abraham's defeat: "[I]n the new generation his grandson will be better equipped for a more constructive life."[154] The *Winnipeg Free Press*'s Joe Gelman began: "You have seen Abraham. You have seen him in his black skull cap, his sharp beard out thrust as he sat in the sun in front of the old frame synagogue."[155] When Laiah was mentioned, it was only in connection with reviewers' shocked reaction to

Abraham as murderer, a critical oversight that dismissed Laiah as "an archetype that foregrounds necessary sacrifice" and sanctioned her death as "beneficial."[156]

Orville Prescott of the *New York Times* read Abraham as "A Patriarch Out of Scripture . . . truly an object of anguished pity."[157] For Winfield Townley Scott of the *New York Herald Tribune*, Abraham embodied Wiseman's reach "for the basic drama of positive and negative forces, of creation and destruction, life and death."[158] The *New Republic*, moreover, commended "the *overt* 'sacrifice' of the book's title" as "one of the most superbly conceived episodes in recent fiction."[159] British reviewers also responded to Wiseman's protagonist. The *Times* celebrated the novel's "noble poetry . . . which gives value to the tragedy that overthrows Abraham" and Moses's final visit to his grandfather as "a promise of new life,"[160] while the *Times Literary Supplement* appreciated "the picture of a whole community of Jews, untouched by surrounding gentile influence . . . as sharp and defined as a Dutch interior."[161]

The success of *The Sacrifice*—coming after a long literary apprenticeship—confirmed Wiseman's "faith in her novel"[162] and the belief that she always had been a writer. Reviewers, impressed by a work that affirms a patriarchal world view and the enduring "rightness" of that view, felt the same love for "*her* Abraham"[163] (italics mine) that Wiseman espoused after she had turned her protagonist to murder. They responded to those elements of the novel that Wiseman sought to refine through painstaking revision: the polished lyricism of her prose; the biblical resonances of character and plot; a compelling patriarch for protagonist; a stunning climax; and a hopeful resolution.

As literary critic Marcia Mack argues, the "biblical story of Abraham—as the site chosen by God out of which the Jewish people would arise—supported the authority of the text's Abraham as patriarch and principal voice of authority and wisdom within the novel."[164]

Conceived, written, and published in the 1950s, *The Sacrifice* posits a world that venerates the male and his progeny. In fact, neither Wiseman nor her reviewers appear to have paid much heed to the prostitute Laiah, who is a necessary but finally dispensable part of the plot of *The Sacrifice*. In accepting that he "took what was not mine to take, . . . what was given to me to hold gently in my hands, to look at with wonder," and in cautioning his grandson, "[w]hen a human being cries out to you, no matter who it is, don't judge him, don't harm him, or you turn away God Himself,"[165] Abraham is partially redeemed. Moses's final reconciliation with his repentant grandfather further softens Abraham's crime and signals the continuing value of Jewish culture and tradition. That little critical attention was given to Laiah, whose murder accommodates that continuity, suggests the patriarchal ideology that informs both the novel and the literary community that received it.

The Sacrifice embraces a set of pervasive, patriarchal assumptions that could ignore the murder of Laiah in favour of extolling Abraham. By extension, its biblical subtext affirms the narrative vision and authority of Abraham that resonated with reviewers and readers and launched Wiseman's career. Moreover, the traditional world view that sanctioned Laiah's "sacrifice" drove Wiseman's rise as writer. The novel went on to win numerous awards, including the Governor General's Award for fiction, the Beta Sigma Phi Sorority Award, and the National Conference of Christian and Jews Brotherhood Award. On the basis of her success, Wiseman was admitted to Yaddo and MacDowell writers' colonies, and she was granted a Canada Foundation Fellowship, a Guggenheim Fellowship, and a Canada Council Arts Scholarship, which took her to New York, where she lived and wrote for a number of years following publication of *The Sacrifice*. Wiseman's simple claim that she wrote "as well as I was able, of what was of most importance to me"[166] belies the labour and energy that she brought to the writing of her first novel. As Kildare Dobbs described *The Sacrifice* prior to publication, it is an "achieved"[167] work of art: shapely and eloquent, it probes the difficult, universal themes of life, death, morality, and human responsibility.

Emboldened by the resounding success of *The Sacrifice*, newly confident in her ability as a writer of international stature and in her relationships with Canadian, American, and British publishers, Wiseman did not rest. Instead, she determined to become a writer of significance, one who challenged herself anew with each project, and she undertook to write a play about European Jews during the Second World War. Although that play, *The Lovebound*, would affect the course of her career in ways she could not anticipate, Wiseman questioned neither the artistic integrity of her writing nor the view of herself as moral witness to her times. As a result of her early triumph as the author of *The Sacrifice*, Wiseman developed an independence that would drive her career, mark its subsequent successes and setbacks, and test those who sought to promote her work.

TWO

Strange, Daring

I am sure Adele Wiseman will produce another book. She will not do it quickly and when she does she will have something more to say.

—Sally Creighton, review of *The Sacrifice*
(CBC Radio, 1956)

TODAY, WISEMAN IS STILL BEST KNOWN for her award-winning first novel. Her second work of fiction, *Crackpot*, did not appear until eighteen years later, in 1974. *Crackpot* was published after more than twenty rejections in the United States and Canada, and its style and content challenged agents and editors, publishers and reviewers alike.

By the time *Crackpot* had begun to germinate in Wiseman's imagination in 1961, she was firmly committed to "writing as a pure vocation, and I wasn't out to sell my purpose by embarking on something I didn't want to do."[1] Conceived and written in the period following the heady success of *The Sacrifice*, *Crackpot* did not appear in print until six years following its completion in 1968. *Crackpot*'s gestation of thirteen years contrasts with the seven years it took Wiseman to write and publish *The Sacrifice*. *The Sacrifice*, moreover, was issued in North America and Great Britain to immediate acclaim, while *Crackpot* did not find a publisher outside Canada and its reception remained mixed.

With Henry Kreisel's *The Rich Man* (1948) and Mordecai Richler's *Son of a Smaller Hero* (1955), *The Sacrifice* was one of the first Canadian novels to explore Jewish life in Canada, and Wiseman returned to this subject in *Crackpot*. Unlike *The Sacrifice*, however, which embraces tradition and endorses a patriarchal world view, *Crackpot* subverts traditional practice with its focus on female experience. Wiseman's second novel turns toward comedy and chronicles the personal history of an obese Jewish prostitute, the daughter of a hunchbacked mother and a blind father, who together flee Russia for Canada. After her mother's death, Hoda supports herself and her father through prostitution, servicing the young men of her North Winnipeg community. The plot hinges on the moral dilemma Hoda faces when her teenaged son (whom she abandons at birth, leaving him in the care of the local Jewish orphanage) visits her for sexual initiation. The choice she faces, between incestuous relations or sexual rejection, leads finally to personal and communal reconciliation.

Crackpot's discursive style and rambling length were intended to accommodate Hoda's dynamic presence and girth. No doubt, that same spontaneity and looseness in the text partly were responsible for the novel's delayed publication and mixed reception. In fact, contemporary response to the novel shows that reviewers could not fully appreciate *Crackpot*—because it differed so strikingly from *The Sacrifice*, the novel that had set the stage for Wiseman's career. Only recently have critics and readers returned to Wiseman's second novel, which is now heralded as a potential "masterpiece"[2] of contemporary

Canadian literature. In today's climate, its daring "complexity"[3] of form and subject is celebrated and *Crackpot* finally is receiving the critical attention it warrants.

Although Hoda did not enter the world until 1974, she was conceived as early as 1961. As Wiseman has described, the character originated with

> a glimpse of somebody. A friend of mine was driving me home once in Winnipeg, and it was quite late at night, and as we passed a certain spot, he said, "There she is." . . . a big, young woman standing on the street corner, and he asked: "Don't you know who she is?" and I said, "No." I had no idea. He gave me a sort of description. He told me that this was a girl who was known to many young men as their initiator into life's mysteries. I had not been acquainted with this fact before. I didn't know the girl, but what remained with me was a kind of visual picture of this great, big, accommodating young woman. . . .[4]

The roots of *Crackpot* lay deeper, however, than "that momentary glimpse of a person"[5] when Wiseman was a young woman in Winnipeg. Between January and June 1961, when she was living in New York, Wiseman likely read in a magazine the lines from the Kabbalah that would become the epigraph to *Crackpot*: "He stored the Divine Light in a Vessel, but the Vessel, unable to contain the Holy Radiance, burst, and its shards, permeated with sparks of the Divine, scattered through the Universe." Two "completely disparate ideas,"[6] prompted by her vision of the prostitute and fragments from the Kabbalah, fused in Wiseman's mind, so that when "I was beginning to write the book . . . I desperately needed that quotation."[7]

Of its source, Wiseman later wrote revealingly and humorously to
Laurence:

> I've been unable to track the quotation down,—know
> only that it's from the Caballah somewhere. So . . . I sent
> out a call via the grapevine, to all the Hebrew scholars
> around. . . . I spent an evening at the Jewish Public Library;
> telephone calls started pouring in, quotations, references,
> discussions, but no exact lead-in on the quot'n I'd seen.
> And some of these people are formidable scholars, know
> the stuff in the original. Was the problem in the original?
> in the translation? Who knows? Finally I was given some
> advice. Make up your own version. . . . And attribute it to
> the Kabbalah: Legends of Creation. So . . . I reproduced a
> quotation as close to the sense of what I'd seen as I could
> remember and now I'm trying to figure out whether I've
> just become a serious contributor to the tradition as well
> as a frivolous writer of fiction.[8]

Inspiration for the novel came swiftly, but it took several years
for "the whole thing . . . to form itself"[9] in Wiseman's imagination.
Later, when immersed in the work, she felt "this great creature strug-
gling to come out of me . . . who's some aspect of my own psyche."[10]
Once the character of Hoda "starting forcing herself out,"[11] Wiseman
understood the lines from the Kabbalah as a framework for the story
that she would write, "as though the metaphor [for creation] was a
very distant world which I was approaching"[12] through writing.

The success of *The Sacrifice* had consolidated Wiseman's commitment to the vocation of writer. Hence, when she turned her attention
to new projects, she intended to continue her practice of taking part-
time employment to support her writing. From 1957 to 1961, she

lived in New York with her friend Amy Zahl, a British photographer whom she had met in London. Supported by several prestigious fellowships, Wiseman researched and wrote *The Lovebound*, a two-act play set in late summer 1939 aboard an ancient freighter crowded with Jews fleeing Europe who are refused refuge in North and South America and are forced to return to the death camps of Germany. Since most reviewers did not know of the failed attempts to produce and publish *The Lovebound*, they incorrectly assumed that *Crackpot* was Wiseman's first large-scale project to follow *The Sacrifice*.

By October 1961, Wiseman was once again in London, where she stayed with Phyllis Gerson, warden of the Stepney Jewish Girls' Club. Wiseman remained in London until April 1962; there she underwent surgery for the removal of benign uterine tumours and recuperated under Gerson's care. In April, she returned to Winnipeg and her family home at 490 Burrows Avenue. Between May 1962 and August 1963, she wrote stories for children—two were published decades later[13]—sold scripts for broadcast on CBC Radio,[14] and marked essays for her alma mater, the Department of English at the University of Manitoba. Her definitive departure from Winnipeg came with the offer of a one-year part-time position in the Department of English at Sir George Williams (now Concordia) University, to teach first-year composition. Wiseman accepted the offer and in September 1963 moved to Montreal, where her elder sister Miriam was a professor of chemistry at McGill University. Shortly after her arrival in Montreal, however, she joined the Department of English at Macdonald College of McGill University, first as lecturer, then assistant professor of English, a full-time teaching position she held from September 1963 until her resignation in April 1969. The move to Montreal facilitated Wiseman's work on *Crackpot*, which she soon began in earnest.

At the age of thirty-five, Wiseman found herself a professor of English and a writer, both satisfying and demanding occupations.

For the first time in her writing life, however, she felt the pull of professional commitments that claimed much of her time and energy. Margaret Laurence well understood the difficulty of balancing the particular demands of the writing life. On 31 December 1964, she wrote to Wiseman:

> Got your letter this morning, and the main thing is—I'm terribly glad etc that you have got going on the novel, even if you have to do it in bits. As a matter of fact I felt what amounted to genuine envy—when you spoke about its being almost automatic writing, and the characters struggling to get out. This is what one always prays will happen . . . Anyway, once the thing has begun to come, nothing can stop it. Just try to unload as many essays on your marker as you possibly can—that's all.[15]

Ironically, over the years Wiseman had worked as a marker for the Department of English at the University of Manitoba—"I could pave the world with the essays I've marked."[16] As she began her work on *Crackpot*—a dense novel that demanded a clear, focussed mind—Wiseman found herself in need of the same assistance she once had provided her former professors.

Finding sufficient time to write was the first challenge Wiseman faced as *Crackpot* began to preoccupy her thoughts. Laurence reassured her friend: "If you have some people (even one) in your novel, who are trying to get out and break through, etc, then you will be okay, however long it takes. I don't know why all this should be so difficult."[17]

Wiseman found the work of writing arduous and exacting. Her previous projects, *The Sacrifice* and *The Lovebound*, each had claimed years of writing and painstaking revision. She could not "dash off a first draft":

There has to be a sentence or two, a paragraph, a cluster, that feels right or I can't go on. So often what I have is a cluster that feels right from here and a cluster that feels right from there. . . . The stuff that doesn't feel right is the crud off the top of your head. It's what everybody else has written, what everyone else has thought *for* you. What I always imagined was if you wanted to be a real writer, you *make things up*—which is nonsense, because people can write very fine books other ways. . . .[18]

Nonetheless, by 17 August 1965, Laurence could write to her friend, "I'm glad your novel is coming along, and in a consecutive way—it doesn't matter if it comes like this, but it is easier to cope with . . . how hard it is to get enough time to oneself."[19] Although "written in a relatively consecutive way"[20]—a technique that may have served the first draft—*Crackpot* eventually underwent substantive revisions.

By the end of the summer, Wiseman had completed the first chapter and was "feeling curiously cheerful":

I seem to have fallen into a prolonged and scarcely inter-ruptible reverie about this new book . . . all kinds of odd things are opening out and filling in for me. The result is that I keep walking in front of cars, tripping over obstacles I only vaguely notice and in general looking to first things first. . . . parts are coming into focus without the general picture being at all clear as yet, and I'm not used to this. I usually have a fair notion of the overall gestalt and have to find out how and why in the writing. . . . if it will only come I don't care how it goes about it; as long as I can have that strange pleasure again I'll put up with the insecurities.[21]

Yiddish novelist Chava Rosenfarb shared a friendship with Wiseman during the latter's years in Montreal, when the two writers enjoyed long talks at a local pub. Although Wiseman would not discuss *Crackpot*, she frequently told her friend "how much she was fascinated" by the character of Hoda. Rosenfarb has speculated: "In a way, she wanted to escape from her work. She felt a contradictory urge: she wanted to write and hated to write. And she found excuses for not writing. . . . Once she sat down and started to work it was okay, but it was difficult to tear herself away from real life. She always created obligations for herself."[22]

During the summer months, free from teaching responsibilities, Wiseman could concentrate on her writing. She found it difficult, however, to maintain her "work pattern"[23] during the academic year and chose to take a one-year (1966–67) unpaid leave from Macdonald College when she was awarded a Quebec Ministry of Cultural Affairs grant-in-aid of her project. Wiseman continued to feel a "perpetual anxiety" that drove her to write, and by 10 July 1966 she reported to Laurence that "Ch. 4 is . . . trying to struggle itself out of my mind."[24] A buoyant Wiseman looked forward to a year of uninterrupted work on her novel; she hoped to complete a first draft before her return to teaching in September 1967.

Wiseman spent part of that year in Miami, Florida, visiting her elder brother Harry, a professor of engineering. Harry and his son Arnold were recovering from the loss of wife and mother, Esther, to cancer on 2 June 1966. True to her intention, Wiseman spent her time writing *Crackpot*, and by 5 May 1967 she felt close enough to completion that she could exclaim to Laurence she would miss "those horrible symptoms . . . when I enter the barrens when this book is done. . . . The 'how to do it' is tough, isn't it? But it's the key, & worth sweating over. It's so lovely when you finally know, & it begins to shape. If the 'how to do' ever stopped bugging one it would be a sure sign that something had gone wrong . . . the beginning of artistic death."[25] Although the summer in Montreal was filled with visitors who arrived for Expo '67 centennial celebrations, by 17 July Wiseman had begun her final chapter: "I have written one sentence of Ch. 14. Luckily it's rather an amusing one, so that I can delude myself . . . into imagining I have a toehold on the chapter."[26]

That same summer she began a relationship with Dmitry Stone, chief biologist with Beak Consultants in Montreal. Stone was born on 10 February 1929 in Alert Bay, British Columbia, to parents of Russian background. Raised and educated in Vancouver, he completed a bachelor's degree in geography and a master's degree in maritime invertebrate zoology at the University of British Columbia. Prior to joining Beak Consultants, Stone had worked for the Manitoba Department of Mines and Natural Resources as a pollution biologist. When he met Wiseman, Stone was separated from his first wife, with whom he had three sons.

Stone's eldest son, Sergei, visited from Vancouver that summer and claimed much of Wiseman's attention. By the end of August 1967, less than two weeks before the start of the academic term, the concluding chapter of *Crackpot* still beckoned. She wrote to Laurence: "I haven't done much writing lately. And yet the darn thing is there, bulging out of my forehead it feels like sometimes, so sometimes in spite of everything I sit down for two hours and bash away. So at least am a few pages into the chapter."[27] *Crackpot* would have to wait, however. The demands of the academic year—following a year-long leave —claimed time and energy, as did Wiseman's relocation with Dmitry Stone to a new apartment at the end of October 1967.

Having returned to teaching and after settling into her living quarters, as "Dmitry cheerfully banged away at making & converting furniture & I banged away at the book every chance I got," Wiseman announced to Laurence on 2 February 1968:

Well, about a week ago I completed the draft. Eureka?
Quasi Eureka? I don't know. I've put it away till the term
is over, as it's most unlikely I'll have much chance to
do anything with it before then. As it stands the thing
is bloody long—nearly 500 pages of 1½ spacing, which
makes each page about equivalent to a printed one. As
for what it's like, I can't really say yet; I haven't read it
through. But this stage is past anyway.[28]

By mid-March, however, Wiseman had reread her manuscript and
decided the final chapter required further work; otherwise, it was
complete. Indeed, the writing "stage" was "past."[29]

AS WISEMAN PREPARED TO SEND "eight legible chapters"[30] of *Crackpot*
to Candida Donadio, a New York literary agent, she could not
have foreseen the extensive revisions that would be required to
effectively market her fiction. Donadio had been recommended
to Wiseman by novelist Joanne Greenberg (aka Hannah Greene,
author of *I Never Promised You a Rose Garden*). Wiseman and
Greenberg had met in 1958 at Yaddo writer's colony in Saratoga
Springs, New York, and they formed a close and enduring friendship. Wiseman felt confident in her second novel and anticipated a
success similar to that she had enjoyed with *The Sacrifice*: easy acceptance by reputable publishers; few editorial revisions; her work
published soon after its completion in typescript. What she did not
consider, however, was the market impact of a twelve-year hiatus
between the publication of a first novel and circulation among editors of her second fiction. In April 1968, when she sent Donadio
representative chapters of *Crackpot*, publishers no longer awaited
Wiseman's work. The promise she once held as the talented author
of *The Sacrifice* had not been fulfilled.

Moreover, editors did not know of the several projects launched in the wake of *The Sacrifice*. Between 1961 and September 1963, while *Crackpot* was "form[ing] itself"[31] in her mind, Wiseman undertook two significant projects. First, she attempted to place her play, *The Lovebound*, which she had begun after *The Sacrifice* and completed in June 1961. Repeated efforts to have the play produced and published failed, however.[32] Eventually, Wiseman had turned her writerly attention to China, where she had hoped to travel with her friend, British photographer Amy Zahl. Wiseman and Zahl had conceived a plan to collaborate on a non-fiction work about China. Wiseman would write the text and Zahl would produce the photographs for the proposed book. In spite of Wiseman's efforts, however, the book was not written.[33]

With *Crackpot*, publishers, editors, and readers had to be courted by Wiseman, a wooing that was not required with her first novel. In every respect—the writing, publication, and reception of the novel—Wiseman's experience with *Crackpot* differed dramatically from her earlier experience with *The Sacrifice*.

Having sent her agent "about half the book (over 200 pages), in an M.S. that had been photocopied . . . on about 5 different occasions & 3 different kinds of machines, in varying degrees of legibility,—a couple of chapters are even photostated,—the printing is white on a mushy grey background,"[34] Wiseman set herself the daunting task of retyping her 500-page novel, a stage Laurence described as "agony."[35] She was reluctant to employ a typist "partly because it makes me nervous, . . . because then I'd have to proof read, which I find a pain in the neck. . . . also because it will cost a fair whack."[36] Laurence counselled otherwise—"pawn the family jewels, kid, and hire a typist"[37]—but her friend was unrelenting: "the typing business really bugs me. . . . I'll be a broken woman by the time, if ever, I reach the end."[38] Wiseman persisted, making minor revisions as she typed, her work completed by mid-August 1968.

Wiseman never was patient with literary agents, and unfortunately the route toward publication of *Crackpot* was long and circuitous. Just one month following submission of her typescript, she already was "annoyed"[39] by Donadio's lack of response. By 29 May 1968, however, the agent had "begun to talk the partial M.S. up to various editors."[40] As she had done with *The Sacrifice*, Wiseman hoped to arrange international publication for her second novel. She informed Donadio of her intention to present *Crackpot* to John Gray, president of Macmillan of Canada, who had issued *The Sacrifice*. At the same time, Donadio offered the novel to Marshall Best of Viking Press, Wiseman's American publisher. Wiseman and her agent hoped to secure an American publisher before approaching British firms.

JOHN GRAY WAS A BOOKMAN and a "natural publisher"[41] who took nationalistic pride in Canada. Temperamentally suited to the task of leader, he "oversaw the most prosperous and successful period"[42] in Macmillan's history. Gray's "boisterous sense of fun" was balanced by his "executive abilities" and the "gift of subordinating his own ambition to the concerns of his writers."[43] Gray's personal desire to be a writer, and his first-hand knowledge of the arduous work that is writing,[44] may have resulted in the generous humility that characterized his correspondence with authors. No doubt, a rare combination of intelligence, perspicacity, and humaneness put Gray "among the leaders of postwar Canadian publishing."[45] Throughout his tenure at Macmillan, he "was one of the most highly regarded publishers in Canada."[46]

Wiseman's relationship with John Gray formed quickly and, despite brief periods of conflict, lasted two decades. Gray was introduced to Wiseman's work through the typescript of *The Sacrifice* that Kildare Dobbs had brought to his attention, and he soon became an ally and advocate for her success. Publisher and writer came to enjoy

John Morgan Gray, c1963.
(Macmillan Company of
Canada fonds, McMaster
University Library)

a relationship of trust that, for Wiseman, would help leaven the disappointments in her career.

In the early years of their association, there was little discord between Wiseman and Gray. In response, however, to a letter in which she asked for clarification on the royalty rate she would receive on *The Sacrifice*, Gray fumed: "[W]hat has happened to your arithmetic? And to your equable disposition? The slightly snide P.S. sounds too much like conventional cracks from disgruntled members of the Canadian Authors' Association and proves only one thing, that you have forgotten my laboured explanation about the difference between royalties on the net and list price."[47] Disturbed by his letter, Wiseman responded that she appreciated Gray's efforts on her behalf and was completely satisfied with her contract. Gray's swift and heartfelt apology—"I am deeply sorry that I spoke as I did. I think your letter caught me on a bad morning—we have had some pretty rough problems recently, and I spoke thoughtlessly and unkindly"[48] —assuaged Wiseman's hurt feelings and buoyed their relationship. Later, when he wrote to congratulate her on winning the Governor General's Award for fiction, Gray assumed a characteristic pose as Wiseman's defender: "There's no surprise about this, of course. We would have started a rebellion if the book hadn't won."[49]

In fact, the sustaining connection between Gray and Wiseman was founded on mutual respect and affection. Throughout the fifties, they exchanged letters that concerned both their professional and personal lives. When, for instance, Wiseman learned from Dobbs that Gray had been ill, she wrote entreating her publisher to care for himself. Gray's answer to Wiseman's expression of solicitude—"Oh, Grandmother what a shaky finger you have! All the better to admonish you with my dear"[50]—revealed the friendship they had come to share. Gray's letter to the Guggenheim Foundation in support of Wiseman's 1957 application described "a significant writer" whose "cheerful self confidence . . . is one of the many remarkable things about her."[51] Dobbs recalled in 1999 that John Gray grew "very fond of Adele. He used to smile whenever her name came up."[52] He also remembered that Gray felt "protective"[53] of Wiseman. In the summer of 1957, for example, when she could not afford to travel from London to Winnipeg to attend the Governor General's Awards ceremony (between 1951 and 1958, a small cash prize of $250 supplemented the Governor General's medal), Gray arranged to cover the cost of an international flight. He also gave her sound advice on applying to the Canada Council for arts grants. After each kindness, Wiseman wrote to acknowledge Gray's generosity.

More notable, however, were the combined efforts of John Gray and Marshall Best to assist Wiseman during the early sixties, when she was completing *The Lovebound*, and later, when she was contemplating a non-fiction book on China. Initially, Dobbs and Gray encouraged

Wiseman in her work on *The Lovebound*. In September 1960, Gray wondered, "How goes the play?"[54] Two months later he rejoiced in the "good news that the end of the play now seems to be in sight and you are cautiously pleased with it. The devotion you have shown should yield the kind of result which will give you satisfaction—at least it should in a just world, and in spite of being unpredictable, this one is sometimes."[55] Despite his expressed hope that "the play roles,"[56] Gray harboured some concern over Wiseman's prolonged engagement with the work. By 1 February 1961, he betrayed himself by writing ironically: "When I think of the dedicated way you have worked at this in the face of discouragement, and I suspect dissuasion, I am filled with awe and admiration—and hope."[57]

Adele Freedman describes Wiseman's decision "to attempt a play at this sensitive point in her career" as

> an act of daring that eventually proved a mistake. It was with *The Lovebound* that Wiseman began in earnest to indulge in an activity that snarled her relationships with editors and publishers . . . [Wiseman] herself calls it "bucking the current." Against the advice of her supporters at Macmillan and Viking, she asserted her determination and wilfulness like the heroine of a Greek tragedy testing the elements.[58]

Malcolm Ross, however, understood Wiseman's resolve to write a play at this stage in her career: "The second big job after a first success is always a trial . . . You don't want to repeat yourself and yet an attempt at something entirely different is always a risk. This is a process of changing gears that most writers go through, and I am sure you will manage it."[59] Unfortunately, Wiseman did not "manage" the play to her satisfaction. In a letter to Best, Gray regretted that "so talented a writer of fiction [was] heading into a blind alley."[60] Unlike Gray, Best wrote directly to Wiseman and "praised the literary qualities" of *The Lovebound* but deplored her "giving so much . . . time and creative energy to the play in the first place."[61] Further, he felt Viking could not "publish unperformed plays."[62]

Convinced at the time that she "was not fulfilling 'the wonderful promise of *The Sacrifice*,'"[63] Gray and Best nonetheless rallied support for Wiseman. In a confidential letter, written in October 1962 following a visit to Winnipeg where Wiseman—"more sadly discouraged than she would readily admit"—had returned to her parents' home, Gray wrote movingly to Best: "My concern is somehow to help provide some encouragement for Adele, if there is any possible basis for it. She has the feeling that the play is likely to die quietly in a corner . . . I am writing . . . to you personally in the hope of causing as little awkwardness or embarrassment as possible—and of course Adele would have no idea that I am writing. . . ." Gray asked if Viking's rejection of *The Lovebound* was irrevocable and whether Best would attempt to circulate the play among "theater people"[64] he knew.

In his frank response to Gray, Best admitted that he had

> some resistance . . . to sympathizing with . . . [Adele] too deeply because I warned her years ago . . . that I thought she was making a terrible mistake. The play is not hopeless as writing, in fact it is the distinguished and beautiful and thoughtful kind of writing one would expect from Adele. It is, however, almost hopeless for theatrical production.[65]

Despite these reservations, Best offered to pass *The Lovebound* on to a theatrical agent. Neither Best nor Gray succeeded, however, in several efforts to promote the play and today it languishes, as Wiseman feared it would, in a quiet, archival corner of Toronto's York University.

Adele Wiseman, July 1961, aboard *S.S. Demosthenes D.* en route to Tokyo.

(Adele Wiseman fonds, Scott Library, York University)

In June 1961, at the suggestion of Margaret Laurence, Wiseman had engaged the services of Willis Kingsley Wing, a literary agent based in New York. An ambitious and successful agent—who wore leg braces as a result of childhood polio—Wing represented several Canadian writers, including Laurence, Robert Kroetsch, and Peter Newman. Wiseman hoped Wing would be able to place her play and she soon sought his assistance on a separate project, the non-fiction book about China. Wiseman and Amy Zahl required advance support for their trip to China and gave Wing a book proposal to circulate among potential publishers. Wiseman received royalty advances for the proposed book of $1000Cdn from Macmillan of Canada, $500US from Harper and Brothers of New York, and £100 from Macmillan of London. In addition, she received royalty advances of $600 from *Maclean's* magazine and $500 from *Weekend Magazine* for articles about China. Although there is no evidence that the initiative was successful, she also appealed

Adele Wiseman, July 1961,
aboard *S.S. Demosthenes D.*
en route to Tokyo.
Photographer: Douglas
Barnaby.

for funds to help finance her trip through the following advertisement
in the *Montreal Star* and the Toronto *Telegram*: "Noted Canadian writer
with publication outlet, journeying to the Orient to create a travel book
for your delight. She will dedicate the book individually to those adventurous spirits who help to make it possible by contributing $500 or
over."[66] Wiseman soon secured free passage to Japan. In June 1961, at
Brooklyn, New York, she boarded the coal-carrying cargo freighter
S.S. Demosthenes D, travelled through the Panama Canal, along the
coast of California, and reached Tokyo on 24 July. Zahl had arrived in
Tokyo prior to Wiseman and had met and become engaged to David
Gottlieb, an American scientist. The couple soon left China for London
to prepare for their marriage, and Wiseman was alone for most of her

subsequent stay in Hong Kong. Between mid–August and October 1961 she resided in Hong Kong, but soon found it necessary to abandon the China project when she was denied entry into the country. In 1961, for political reasons, China would admit few foreign visitors.

While in Hong Kong, Wiseman was forced to face two crushing disappointments. First, Wing's response to *The Lovebound* arrived in August—upon arrival in Tokyo, Wiseman had sent him a revised copy of her play—and it was entirely negative. Wing found *The Lovebound* "overburdened with dialogue; it is just plain too talky. . . . some of the central threads . . . become less and less visible, so that the real direction of the play in terms of some of the principal characters becomes too blurred."[67] Second, since Wiseman and Zahl were refused admission to China, they could not proceed with their proposed book.

Throughout her "wild junket to China"[68] and its unfortunate outcome, Gray was cautiously supportive of Wiseman. When she requested additional support, Gray boosted Macmillan's royalty advance from $500 to $1000, although he "would rather make it $750. or $500."[69] When she offered to write a book about her unsuccessful attempt to reach China, Gray was encouraging: "It is a little hard to know what the revised book may consist of but if in time you see a book in what you are doing, we would expect to like the result."[70] In fact, an enthusiastic Dobbs reported "that he and John Grey [sic] both felt they'd stake their lives on your turning up finally with something very good from that trip."[71] One year later, however, in October 1962, Best wrote this lament to Gray:

> We have also seen the three chapters of the book on the abortive China trip and while it is pleasant and entertaining, it is completely pointless as far as book publication is concerned. We have had to send discouraging word about this also through [Willis] Wing but have said that

if we like the complete book when we see it, and if you should by any chance be going ahead with it, the question could be reopened. We too would like to do everything within reason to encourage Adele's realization of her great promise, which seems to have gone so far astray.[72]

Unlike Macmillan, however, Viking had not issued Wiseman a royalty advance for her book on China. Regardless, a generous Gray preferred not to press Wiseman: "I know . . . [the advance] is on her mind probably more than is good for her work, but I have tried to reassure her a bit."[73]

When Gray offered a suggestion, however—that she might attempt to rework *The Lovebound* as a novel—Wiseman refused flatly, saying that the form suited the content of the work. To the consternation of publishers and editors, Wiseman clung tenaciously to the principle that revision would defile her writing. Wiseman's stubborn refusal to amend the play may have veiled her unwillingness to concede a painful truth: that her own artistic judgement was flawed and that she had spent five, long years writing a play less dramatic than cerebral that included extended passages of dialogue, such as the following by Hitzig Komish, a character who recalls a lost opportunity to escape the fate that awaits him in Germany:

> I had played my way past every trap and obstacle to the
> very core and heart of hell. The heroic moment, the per-
> ilous encounter a man dreams of. There stood one of the
> overlords of the underworld, bribed, by my efforts, to a
> semblance of momentary courtesy. Here was I, my prize
> before me, ready to seize him and make the audacious
> leap from the grave to freedom. Just like the manuals! Oh
> those blessed manuals that teach me how men have lived,

how men can live, how men should live. Triumph indeed
to be a member of the manuals, albeit without portfolio,
as yet unsung, but something still of a redeemer of Cain.
Why is it then that all I could think of was how badly
I needed to leave the room? Oh I had such a devil of a
cramp! "Let's quit already," I kept thinking. "Let's have a
break. Let's make borrows. Don't talk so much. Just show
me where . . . Ask me, go on ask me, "'Wouldn't you like
to wash your hands? Powder your nose?' Please!" And I
was furious . . . because I didn't have the courage to ask
the Obercommandant to let me use his private facilities,
because I was afraid that if I got so intimate he might ask
for my credentials and want to examine my papers.[74]

As Gray and Best understood, it would have been impossible to
successfully mount *The Lovebound*, a four-hour play set aboard a ship,
with little action and much discussion, no matter how evocative the
dialogue. Obsessed as she was with its central idea that the world
would sanction the demise of all Jews, Wiseman, however, could not
turn away from her play.

Today, it is difficult to accept Wiseman's fervent commitment to
The Lovebound, especially in light of its repeated rejection by agents
and publishers who understood the contemporary market for dramatic work. The play evokes a potentially redemptive moment in
1939, when a significant number of European Jews could have been
rescued from concentration camps. In fact, Wiseman was unable to
assimilate the world's lack of response to the great number of Jews
who sought succour in various countries prior to the onset of war in
Europe. Nor could she accept that her play, which explores a profound
moment in recent history, would leave its readers cold. In the end, her
insistence on the artistic integrity of *The Lovebound* reflected a personal

and moral commitment to its subject—the tragic loss of European Jewry during the Second World War—and a general disregard for the market conditions that might facilitate its production.

In addition to serving as conduit between Wiseman and Best, Gray communicated with Willis Wing over the China book and, later, when she severed her contract with Wing, he helped ease the tension between author and agent. Gray explained to Wing that Wiseman "had come to some sort of dead-end," and that a "change may be a good thing for her."[75] When Wing responded that his efforts to serve his client had been misunderstood and underappreciated, Gray's thoughtful and measured letters sought to re-establish equilibrium between the agent and Wiseman.

In November 1962, Gray had suggested that Wiseman take a job in which she "might get deeply involved."[76] Practical even when she appeared otherwise, Wiseman did not balk at his advice. In all likelihood, she recognized the need to seek paid employment, since, by 1962, her writing career had slowed considerably, and she accepted Gray's offer of a new writing project.

Old Markets, New World was conceived with Wiseman in mind. On 21 August 1963, Gray sent Wiseman copies of Joe Rosenthal's drawings of Toronto's Kensington Market and wondered "what kind of text—how long and of what nature exactly—would with them make a book."[77] Attracted by the drawings, Wiseman agreed to supply an essay on old city markets to accompany Rosenthal's work. Although she procrastinated in her usual manner, the piece Wiseman delivered to Macmillan evoked "the now vanished market on North Main in Winnipeg"[78] and was described as "excellent" by reader Jim Bacque: "Adele has seen exactly what's needed, and given it."[79] Wiseman appreciated the opportunity to participate in the joint project and wrote to compliment Gray on the beautiful design of *Old Markets, New World*. The book was awarded a Bronze Medal at the 1964 Leipzig Book Fair.

Four years later, in the summer of 1968, however, Wiseman faced the first and most painful rejection of *Crackpot*. That August, she heard from Donadio, who reported on Viking's refusal to publish the work. Marshall Best had written:

> To have this new script arrive was tantalizing. It is apparent that she has been working away at it slowly for years. . . . The material is as authentic as it was before and the central characters are moving and effective. Meanwhile, however, times have changed for this kind of story, which might have seemed fresh and important a decade or so ago, now seems too familiar. The painstaking and leisurely style also seems somewhat out-of-date.[80]

If, however, Wiseman agreed to substantially cut her work and Macmillan were to publish the novel, Best "would be glad to see it again."[81]

As she herself often admitted to editors and fellow writers, Wiseman took a "rather intransigent approach to advice."[82] Not only was she angry—"yours truly is a has-been without hardly even having was'd!"[83]—Wiseman was disheartened by Viking's dismissal of her work as no longer relevant or interesting. The first rejection, coming from an important American publisher who had once readily accepted her fiction, plunged Wiseman into a state of dejection: "I am really chilled to the marry-bones. Why bother writing? Why go to all the trouble to try to find my voice, when it's been heard before and no longer seems as fresh[?]"[84] Best's rejection of *Crackpot* was especially painful for Wiseman.

As soon as she received the disappointing news, Laurence cabled a message intended to reassure her friend. Instead, the message provided the much needed balm of humour, for the telegram was delivered in garbled form as "VIKING IS IN SPAIN TRANOPF LETTER FOLLOWS LOVE MARGARET."[85] The telegram ought to have read "Viking is insane Try Knopf." The letter that followed celebrated Wiseman's commitment to her particular vision and the quality of her work (Laurence had read two chapters of *Crackpot* in May 1967) but nothing dispelled the "first spasm of rage, injured pride, perhaps a little despair"[86] as much as Laurence's misconveyed message. In fact, the forty-year friendship Wiseman shared with Laurence helped sustain both women during such times of crisis.

That *Crackpot* had difficulty finding a publisher may not have come as a complete surprise, since it never had been Wiseman's intention to write the same kind of novel as *The Sacrifice*. Wiseman soon recognized, however, that agents and editors expected her to exceed the excellence of her initial effort, a challenge for any writer whose first novel meets with great success. Further, in form and subject matter, *Crackpot* could be read to subvert *The Sacrifice*, a highly polished, serious text. The scope and humour of *Crackpot* likely caught its first readers—the agents, editors, and publishers to whom it was submitted—off guard.

Soon Wiseman was "back in reasonably fighting mood"[87] and could respond temperately to the next rejection from Harper and Row, on the grounds that "the craziness [in *Crackpot*] simply overpowers the nice things & one worries about the success of the novel."[88] Wiseman was confused by publishers' responses to her second novel. Although she understood how difficult it was to judge her own work—its "seriousness, depth, value, staying power, honesty, grasp, complexity"[89]—she had anticipated less difficulty in placing *Crackpot*, which she regarded as a departure from and worthy successor to *The Sacrifice*. She rallied and remained convinced of its integrity.

Over the next five years, however, *Crackpot* would be rejected by seventeen American publishing houses, as well as by five other British and three other Canadian publishers.[90] Disturbed by the poor response to her work, Wiseman sought the advice of her colleague Desmond Cole, chair of the Department of English at Macdonald College, and Malcolm Ross, whose critical insight and honesty she trusted. On 30 December 1968, she sent Ross a copy of *Crackpot*. Although he had reservations about its tone and treatment of sex, Ross felt *Crackpot* was worthwhile:

> It is a powerful and very moving novel. Certainly you have lost nothing of the wonderful sense of people and place that comes through so strikingly in The Sacrifice. . . . all your people have their due degree of flesh and blood. . . . And there is the marvellous double irony of the father-daughter handling of the daughter's "professional" life. . . . I can't believe that you won't get a strong publisher.[91]

Heartened by Ross's careful reading and Cole's admiration for her work, Wiseman finally was encouraged to submit *Crackpot* to Macmillan of Canada and by 26 March 1969 she had sent John Gray a copy of her long-awaited novel. Her relationship with Gray would soon be tested.

MACMILLAN'S STINGING REBUFF was as searing as Viking's earlier rejection of *Crackpot* and was softened only by the birth of Wiseman's daughter, Tamara Reesa Esther Bliss Stone, on 26 June 1969. Wiseman had resigned from Macdonald College in April 1969 and had relocated with her family to the greater Toronto area where Dmitry Stone had been transferred by Beak Consultants. Wiseman and Stone celebrated the birth of their daughter by marrying on New Year's Eve 1969.

Macmillan's readers evaluated *Crackpot* through April and May and their responses were mixed. Janice Patton was impressed by the character of Hoda; she recommended the book for publication, with some revision to the second part of the novel and its ending.[92] Two other readers acknowledged that "[l]iking or not liking this particular novel is ultimately much a matter of the reader's temperament. . . . It is either a tour de force or a brave failure";[93] nonetheless, each criticized *Crackpot* as being gangling and prolix.

As her first publisher, Gray welcomed the opportunity to read Wiseman's second novel. Unwilling as he was to reject it, he could not disagree with his readers' assessments of the work, however. In a letter to Wiseman dated 27 May 1969, which included copies of two readers' reports, Gray wrote that *Crackpot* lacked interest:

> There's no point in elaborating my viewpoint because it is covered by what is here . . .
>
> I'm deeply sorry . . .
>
> If the sum total of our readings was more encouraging, I would feel happier about urging you to revise. As it is, I suspect you don't yourself now like the book enough to enjoy revision. But I hate the idea of your giving up fiction . . .
>
> Meanwhile I'm sad at giving you this news.[94]

Stunned by Gray's assumption that she would submit to Macmillan's evaluation of her novel, Wiseman turned to Margaret Laurence. On 12 June 1969, she confided in her friend:

> I'm afraid I'm incurably pig headed about my own literary judgment. I am not incapable of responding to someone whose judgment I respect, but nothing I read in reports

or John's letter aroused much by way of respect. I am still stunned, for instance, to find that my characters are grotesque. . . . I must simply gird myself to what may turn out to be the total response of publishers, in which case tant pis.[95]

On 17 July 1969, after she had taken time to consider her response, Wiseman wrote mildly to inform Gray that she remained convinced of the value of her work.[96]

In an effort to elaborate his position and possibly to assuage Wiseman, Gray explained that his "good intelligent readers" were admirers of her work. He insisted, however, "that the onus is on the writer to interest, and to be understood by 'average' readers." Gray was certain that Wiseman had lost perspective on *Crackpot* because it was "written in pieces over a number of years."[97]

Wiseman was hurt by Gray's comments, "all done with earnest good will and sincere friendship," and found their exchange of letters "killingly depressing."[98] While she may have had naïve expectations when she sent her typescript to Macmillan, she was not prepared for Gray's rough rejection of her work. Although Gray's letter of 12 August 1969 was conciliatory ("If after Margaret Laurence and others have read your book, and you have thought more about it all, let us talk some more"[99]), Wiseman did not resubmit her revised novel to Macmillan. Instead, she focussed on her new daughter and her writing, and determined to "get over"[100] her depression.

Mordecai Richler had accepted an excerpt from *Crackpot* for an anthology of Canadian writing he was editing—it would appear in 1970[101]—but Wiseman was growing "heartsick"[102] over her novel's failure to find a publisher. As she would proclaim later, rather trenchantly: "E=MC squared means that the Excellence of a truly original work of art is equal to the product of the initial recoil of Most editors and Critics."[103] When Candida Donadio could not place *Crackpot* in the United States, Wiseman turned her attention to the smaller Canadian market and hired literary agent Matie Molinaro. In 1950, Molinaro had pioneered the Toronto-based Canadian Speakers' and Writers' Service, Canada's first literary agency.

It was Phyllis Grosskurth, however, professor of English at the University of Toronto and a friend since June 1966, who was instrumental in bringing *Crackpot* to Longman Canada. Grosskurth's biography of John Addington Symonds had been published by Longman in Britain,[104] and she approached its Canadian branch on Wiseman's behalf and "talked Longman into accepting the book."[105] Longman agreed, but only if Grosskurth were to act as editor and persuade Wiseman to cut the novel.[106] On 17 July 1970, Longman made an offer to publish *Crackpot* and paid Wiseman a royalty advance of $2000.[107]

In September 1970, Wiseman proclaimed to Laurence: "The agent tells me that she & Longmans [sic] are close to an agreement, & that the contract should be ready any day now. I've done all I want to do on the book, so there is a real possibility I'll be rid of it soon!"[108] Molinaro negotiated with Longman on behalf of her client.[109] Wiseman, however, soon announced to Grosskurth that she would not consent to the editorial arrangement stipulated by Longman because, as Grosskurth stated, "she considered my views very prudish."[110] In fact, Grosskurth claimed she never was clear about her role as editor of *Crackpot*: "All I was concerned about was getting a publisher"[111] for the novel. In the interim, Longman sought an American publisher. In March 1972, however, after a long and frustrating delay and without a positive response from any of their affiliate houses in the United States, Longman allowed its contract to lapse on the grounds that *Crackpot*'s length made it a risky undertaking.

Following this second rejection by a Canadian publisher, Wiseman heeded an earlier suggestion made by Laurence (in 1969 Laurence had read and suggested revisions to the first draft of *Crackpot*) that she submit her novel to House of Anansi Press. The typescript that landed on Shirley Gibson's desk at Anansi—sent by Molinaro on the author's behalf—"contained, along with some terrific writing, 'an incredible amount of crap.'"[112] Thus began the final and substantive revisions to the novel.

Wiseman described the first draft of *Crackpot* as follows: "It originally had a very rigid structure. I had been so enamoured by the idea of the architectonic, I had conceived *Crackpot* as two parallel stories: Hoda and her son. . . . So, in that first version, there was a lot of the boy, his experiences, etc."[113] It took advice from Margaret Atwood, who was senior editor at Anansi, to spur Wiseman toward necessary and effective revision. By 26 May 1973, Wiseman was completing revisions to her novel in preparation for a meeting with Shirley Gibson and James Polk of Anansi, who were "eager to have the author of *The Sacrifice* on its list."[114]

In several later interviews, Wiseman expressed gratitude to Atwood for the perceptive advice that drove her "to change direction and abandon the original project."[115] Atwood felt "that there wasn't enough balance between the two main characters"[116] in *Crackpot*. Significantly, Wiseman attended to Atwood's comment that there might be a way out of "the rigidity of my pre-manufactured parallel structure."[117] In a telephone conversation, Atwood had touched the right chord. Wiseman says,

> [A]fter talking to her I went around for a couple of weeks mumbling to myself. And then I was standing at the sink doing the dishes one day and . . . it suddenly occurred to me that instead of laboriously creating the parallels, I could use the uncle and have . . . [Hoda] really live her perceptions of the boy's life through the uncle's stories.[118]

By incorporating these changes—"not a great deal of work, just a different way of getting where I want to go"[119]—Wiseman cut approximately seventy pages from her typescript and completed the final revisions to *Crackpot*.

By mid-September 1973, an optimistic Wiseman had resubmitted her novel to Anansi. Apparently, however, the revisions were not satisfactory and, following "a heated argument with Gibson, Wiseman put down the phone . . . and withdrew her manuscript."[120] Angry and frustrated, Wiseman faced her third rejection by a Canadian publisher and the real possibility that *Crackpot* might remain unpublished.

As early as April 1969, Laurence had suggested that Wiseman send her novel to her publisher and friend Jack McClelland of McClelland and Stewart. Wiseman had been hesitant to submit her work to McClelland after the early misunderstanding regarding publication of *The Sacrifice*, where she offered that book to Macmillan despite already having been approached by Malcolm Ross on behalf of McClelland and Stewart. When she heard of Anansi's rejection of *Crackpot*, Laurence was moved to take matters into her own hands.

Laurence wrote to McClelland, explaining her friend's difficulty in placing *Crackpot*. Should McClelland decide to publish the novel, she stipulated as a condition of acceptance that revisions would not be required and only editorial suggestions permitted. In answer to Laurence, McClelland wrote to Wiseman on 12 October 1973, a letter remarkable for its generous and open spirit:

> I don't think it is appropriate for me to comment on what has taken place, but I would like to say that we would be delighted to become your publishers in Canada. I don't harbour even the slightest grudge about THE SACRIFICE. I thought I had explained that to you before. My only feeling was one of great regret because we should have

liked to have been your publishers. It didn't work out
that time—which is too bad but which is water under the
bridge—but hopefully it can work out now.[121]

McClelland's encouragement would be impressive even if he had not
known of *Crackpot*'s troubling history. His offer to become Wiseman's
publisher during a period of crisis in her career affirms McClelland
and Stewart's legendary commitment to Canadian authors.

From its founding in 1906, McClelland and Stewart had set out to
publish writing by and for Canadians. Throughout the twentieth century, the company was synonymous with Canadian publishing and its
roster of eminent writers included novelists Gabrielle Roy, Margaret
Laurence, Mordecai Richler, and Margaret Atwood; poets Irving
Layton, Al Purdy, and Leonard Cohen; and popular writers Pierre
Berton, Farley Mowat, and Peter Newman. When Jack McClelland
joined his father's firm in 1946, he brought dynamism and vision to
his work with authors and their books. If he faced financial difficulties over the course of his career, difficulties that finally forced the
sale of the company in January 1986, he also experienced professional
exhilaration and the pleasure of knowing that his efforts enriched the
lives of authors, readers, and the field of publishing in Canada. In
fact, if not for the perspicacity of McClelland, a "patient, tactful man
willing to do almost anything to make an author happy,"[122] *Crackpot*
likely would not have been published during its author's lifetime. That
Wiseman rallied to pursue other projects and continued to regard herself as a serious writer was due in large part to the gracious spirit of
Jack McClelland.

McClelland invited Wiseman to submit *Crackpot* to McClelland
and Stewart: "[S]end it marked to my personal attention so that I will
know when it arrives . . . and I promise you that we will deal with it
so quickly it will amaze you."[123] McClelland was true to his word. On

29 October 1973, before his readers had completed their evaluations of the novel, he wrote to Wiseman announcing his intention to publish the novel. McClelland outlined the general terms of a publishing agreement that included a royalty advance of $2000.[124] Although he felt the novel "might benefit from some excision," he did not insist on changes and looked forward to publishing Wiseman's "extraordinarily fine book."[125]

McClelland's single objection was to the work's title, which he found "totally inappropriate and also extremely limiting."[126] In a passionate exchange of letters written between October 1973 and May 1974, McClelland hoped to convince Wiseman of the need to change her title to *Hoda*. Wiseman, however, would not concede to McClelland's view that the colloquial meaning of "crackpot" would cast a shadow over her serious novel and hurt potential sales. McClelland argued: "[*Crackpot*] is a symbol of a lightweight book at best and at worst, a symbol of an experimental book in a [narrow] subject area."[127] Wiseman suggested "Hoda's Tale" as subtitle, but McClelland did not feel it would improve the book's prospects and they settled magnanimously on *Crackpot*. Despite past rejections, Wiseman remained convinced of the integrity of her novel, as shown by her ardent defence of its title.

Between October and December 1973, McClelland and Stewart continued its assessment of Wiseman's text. Readers Greg Gatenby and Lily Poritz Miller felt it was too long, and this view was corroborated by editors Linda McKnight and Anna Porter. Porter agreed with McClelland, however: "[I]t's a very fine piece of work, a highly entertaining novel and could and should be a critical and commercial success."[128]

Given the circumstances surrounding *Crackpot*—McClelland's early acceptance of the novel and his unwillingness to alienate Wiseman—an external evaluation was sought from editorial consultant Diane Mew. In a thorough, three-page report, Mew outlined suggestions for revision that might improve the focus of *Crackpot*, "a powerful, gripping piece of writing, eminently publishable."[129] Apparently, a summary of Mew's report was sent to Wiseman, who was protected from harsh criticism by McClelland and Stewart. In her letter to Wiseman, Mew proposed three kinds of revision to the novel: changes in punctuation; minor deletions throughout the typescript; and substantial altering of the final chapter. Appended to the letter were nine pages of detailed notes. Despite McClelland and Stewart's apprehension, Wiseman welcomed Mew's comments and agreed to many of the changes she suggested, in particular to conclude the novel with the penultimate rather than the final chapter. By March 1974, the revisions were completed and McClelland could proceed with confidence.[130] McClelland's efforts ensured that *Crackpot* received careful editorial attention.

Having accepted *Crackpot* for publication, McClelland soon asked to read Wiseman's two unpublished plays, *The Lovebound* and *Testimonial Dinner*, the latter a brief, three-act play completed in 1974 that includes Sir John A. Macdonald and Louis Riel among its various characters. Although he cautioned, "[w]e are not all that interested in publishing plays," McClelland reasoned that *The Lovebound* "is not a normal play and it is just possible that we should do it as a book."[131] Although he chose not to publish either work, McClelland's readers gave Wiseman's drama serious consideration. For Bill Teskey, *The Lovebound* was "static" but it made "fine reading."[132] Lily Poritz Miller and Wailan Low, who went on to practise law and later was the partner of poet Earle Birney, described it as unoriginal and agreed that it lacked interest and structure: "the setting never changes . . . [and] there is almost no action."[133] The same readers did not find *Testimonial Dinner* any more satisfying: "[C]haotic and directionless,"[134] its "themes are laid, like eggs, but never hatched."[135]

Published on 28 September 1974, *Crackpot* was promoted in Toronto and Montreal as "a richly textured novel, resonant with myth, superstition and reality, echoing . . . the same divine spark that Hoda yearns so earnestly to share with the world."[136] Four thousand copies were printed at a production cost of $9769.73. Book of the Month Club was granted Canadian book-club rights to *Crackpot* for a five-year period beginning 14 August 1974. In December 1974 the novel was designated an "Alternate Selection" of Book of the Month Club, Canada; by December 1979 the club had sold 955 of its 1000 copies.[137] Wiseman received seventy-five per cent (instead of the usual fifty per cent) of Book of the Month Club royalties received from *Crackpot*.

Having received a pre-publication copy of *Crackpot*, Wiseman wrote to McClelland on 7 September 1974. She praised the book's design and noted an unfortunate misprint on the final page where "previence" was substituted for "prurience" in the sentence, "'PRURI-ENCE,' she held out her arms, a true bride." In the galleys of *Crackpot*, "pudenda" was substituted for "prurience," an error Wiseman had corrected. McClelland's response was immediate. He prepared an errata slip for each copy of the book; a tipped-in page replaced the incorrect page in all copies required for immediate distribution; and McClelland promised to correct the error in reprintings of the novel.[138]

Crackpot sold slowly and the first impression was not sold out until 1978. As general editor of McClelland and Stewart's New Canadian Library (NCL) reprint series, it had been Malcolm Ross's intention to issue *Crackpot* as an NCL title in 1978. Hence, in January 1978, *Crackpot* appeared as volume 144 in the series, with an introduction by Margaret Laurence. Two months later, in an effort to reduce the remaining stock of hardcover copies and to make way for the paperback issue of the novel, 750 copies were sold to W.H. Smith bookstores. On 1 April 1979, 2226 paperback copies of *Crackpot* were reprinted at a production cost of $2598.44.[139] A new NCL edition was published in 1989.

McClelland believed the hardcover "should have succeeded in selling more copies"[140] and anticipated an increased sale of the novel in paperback. Priced at $10.00 in hardcover, the book may have been too costly for most readers. Indeed, as reviewer Bess Kaplan noted ironically, its price likely limited "sales to that section of readership which likes to be up on the latest conversation-piece—and can afford the luxury."[141] Both McClelland and Wiseman were gratified, however, when *Crackpot* received the Canadian Booksellers Association Book Award, as well as the Montreal Jewish Public Library's J.I. Segal Foundation Award. After a prolonged gestation and an unfortunate delay in publication, publisher and author appreciated praise for *Crackpot*. For Wiseman especially, commendation was a welcome anodyne to the criticism that had been heaped upon her work by editors and publishers. Finally, *Crackpot* was available to the public and Wiseman eagerly awaited its response to her second novel.

MARGARET LAURENCE AND BARBARA AMIEL were *Crackpot*'s first reviewers and their contrary readings—in the *Globe and Mail* and the *Toronto Star*, respectively—appear to have set the stage for its reception. Laurence's friendship with Wiseman may have coloured her positive review of *Crackpot*. She praised the novel's "sustained drama, epic in its scope and vision,"[142] and celebrated the character of Hoda as fully alive. For Amiel, though, the work's "powerful moments" were "paralyzed or dissipated by flabby writing."[143] With the exception of a few strident voices—the *Lethbridge Herald* reviewer found *Crackpot* revoltingly pornographic[144]—the media response to the novel was largely positive, however. Although many noted its length and some suggested it ought to have been edited more carefully, most reviewers welcomed the appearance of Wiseman's novel after a long interval.

Wiseman felt that Laurence's evaluation of *Crackpot* had a broader impact than Amiel's negative comments, and a sampling of reviews from across the country corroborates this impression. In separate radio reviews, Edgar Bennett in Halifax described the novel as "irrepressibly human" (CBC),[145] while Isobel McKenna in Ottawa called it "one of the more important novels in recent literature" (CFMO, CFRA, CJET).[146] In St. John's, Ann Crosby appreciated the work's "folkloric overtones" (*Evening Telegram*);[147] David Legate of Montreal enjoyed the novel's "exquisitely handled sense of humor" (*Montreal Star*);[148] a reviewer in Saskatoon celebrated Hoda as "a living, breathing character" (*Star-Phoenix*);[149] and, further west, she "is at middle age, still big with love—the crackpot" (*New Westminster*).[150] Repeatedly, Hoda was felt as a "life-force" (*Canadian Reader*),[151] and reviewers declared it "would be a pity if a sequel [to *Crackpot*] were to take another 18 years" (*Time*).[152]

Several key reviews, however, may have influenced potential readers. The Montreal *Gazette* dismissed *Crackpot* as "embarrassing,"[153] and the *Winnipeg Free Press* questioned Laurence's judgement: "It will be very surprising . . . if this novel receives either . . . popular or critical acclaim."[154] George Woodcock, respected man of letters, added his voice to the fray. This "blowsy, picaresque book" is "only kept afloat by its humor" (*Maclean's*),[155] he claimed, and Peter Stevens, professor of English at the University of Windsor, commented: "Despite its strong scenes, its fine delineation of major and minor characters, somehow the ironic mode keeps the novel at a distance from the reader. Too often it resorts to reported speech when an incident demands to be presented in the words of the participant" (*Windsor Star*).[156] Although Laurence would soon report that a student acquaintance had read *Crackpot* "and was knocked out by the character of Hoda,"[157] for a number of reasons the novel did not attract as wide an audience as *The Sacrifice*.

Unlike *The Sacrifice*, which was issued simultaneously in North America and Great Britain, *Crackpot* was available only in Canada, which limited its potential audience. To its further detriment, *Crackpot* was expensive, the most costly of several novels issued in 1974 by McClelland and Stewart. At $10.00, *Crackpot* competed unfavourably with other McClelland and Stewart titles: Matt Cohen's *The Disinherited* ($8.95), Margaret Laurence's *The Diviners* ($8.95), and Sinclair Ross's

Sawbones Memorial ($7.95), for example. In general, works of fiction were priced below $10.00. Audrey Thomas's novel *Blown Figures* was published by Talonbooks and cost $4.50, for instance; Alice Munro's collection of short stories, *Something I've Been Meaning to Tell You*, was issued by McGraw-Hill Ryerson and sold for $7.95. Moreover, a paperback issue was delayed until 1978, four years following *Crackpot*'s appearance in hardcover, when media attention had long turned to more recent fiction. Finally, its tiny typeface was exceedingly difficult to read and *Crackpot* was not reset until 1989, when McClelland and Stewart published a New Canadian Library paperback edition with a more legible typeface.

Although several reviewers claimed *Crackpot* compared favourably with Laurence's *The Diviners*, a long novel as well, the slower pace of Wiseman's work may have tried the patience of some readers. The CBC's Robert Weaver also confirmed Jack McClelland's suspicion: "[T]he one unreserved criticism I have about the book is its title. The word 'crackpot' seems to me inadequate to describe the abundance of life in the novel, and I know from experience of simply showing the book to several people that it isn't going to do much to attract readers."[158]

Fellow writer and friend Sylvia Fraser observed that Wiseman "received a lot of criticism over the second book . . . because it wasn't the first book."[159] As literary critic Marcia Mack explains, unlike *The Sacrifice, Crackpot* "accommodates, even privileges, the viewpoint of the prostitute. . . . [which] goes a long way toward explaining Canadian critics' difficulty in responding to the work."[160] Readers who associated Wiseman with her refined delineation of Abraham, fallen patriarch of *The Sacrifice*, were not prepared for the rollicking prostitute who presided over *Crackpot* and who regularly

> gave way to the pressure of her thoughts, and went off,
> after a light-hearted beginning, into long, discursive

monologues, noting the restiveness of her captive audience
after a while, but unable to stop herself just yet from trying
to hunt down and capture the truth towards which her
unwinding words seemed to beckon, perennially teasing
her to the perennially incomplete revelation of words, and
yet more words.[161]

By 1974, the story of lower-class, Jewish immigrants to North
America had become familiar and, as one reviewer put it, Hoda was
"just a little too much to take" (*Calgary Herald*).[162] Too, Wiseman's
rendering of Winnipeg as inhospitable to newcomers, her novel's
loose style and subversive handling of incest, presented here between
a knowing mother—who is "nonvictim and nonmartyr"[163]—and her
naïve son, likely offended the modest sensibilities of proud Canadian
readers. That six years earlier the same reviewers and readers had
responded more temperately to the sexually explicit *Beautiful Losers*,
Leonard Cohen's contentious novel also published by McClelland and
Stewart, may point to a general bias against *Crackpot*—and, by extension, its author—for its unconventional treatment of female sexuality.[164]
Publication confirmed what many editors and publishers had sensed
earlier—that *Crackpot* would appeal to a select audience who could
appreciate its indomitable protagonist and daring execution.

As early as December 1974, reviewer A.J. Arnold remarked pre-
sciently: "[*Crackpot* is] a controversial novel and must encouter [sic]
a mixed reception in some quarters. . . . This book will gain in
acceptance and grow in importance as time passes" (*Western Jewish
News*).[165] In fact, the first sustained evaluation of the novel, written
by Kenneth Sherman, appeared in autumn 1974 and it soon was followed by several scholarly reviews.[166] Critic Helene Rosenthal, for
example, proclaimed: "I'm going all out against my carefully acquired
academic caution to recommend *Crackpot* as the most alive, daring,

and tempestuously human literary creation in Canadian storytelling"
(*Canadian Literature*).[167] Rosenthal's response to the novel was unique
in its exuberance alone. Like most reviewers, the majority of *Crackpot*'s
earliest critics praised Wiseman for her significant achievement. But
despite positive attention from reviewers and critics alike, *Crackpot*'s
reach was not wide. Hoda's spontaneity, the vagaries of her unfet-
tered life, and Wiseman's untethered style challenged those who recalled the order and unadorned elegance of *The Sacrifice*. Moreover,
while Abraham finally atones for his crime of murder, Hoda is never
judged harshly for her crimes of prostitution and incest and eventually is rewarded with the rejuvenative love of Lazar. As Marian Engel
understood in 1975: "Wiseman's a strange writer. She doesn't fit in,
any more than Hoda does. She is prolix and life-loving, immensely
strong. . . . There's no one in the country to touch her unashamed
femininity and Jewishness. It's a very odd combination and it's mag-
ical."[168] Upon publication in 1974, while many reviewers applauded
Crackpot—a "strange, daring and triumphant novel"[169]—others felt
estranged from Wiseman's text.

In recent years, however, several critics have read the novel anew.
Since the early 1990s, scholars have re-examined Hoda's struggle for
autonomy from post-colonial and feminist perspectives, for example.
They probe issues of class, ethnicity, and anti-Semitism that lie at the
heart of her experience, and they understand her spirited character as
a rare example of a sex worker who is treated with empathy by her
creator.[170] Ruth R. Wisse, professor of Yiddish and comparative literature at Harvard University, includes *Crackpot* in the canon of modern
Jewish writing.[171] In addition, *Crackpot* is taught regularly in university
departments of English, women's studies, and Jewish studies, and is
reaching a new generation of readers.

Readers who admired Hoda did not wait long for another work
by Wiseman. Wiseman's daring artistry and belief in the redemptive

value of art soon bore new fruit in a work of non-fiction that tested her abilities in profound ways, and whose central character was her own indomitable mother, Chaika Waisman.

THREE

A Genuine Creation

WISEMAN'S THIRD SUBSTANTIAL WORK, *Old Woman at Play*, a memoir of her mother and her mother's craft of doll making, was published four years after *Crackpot*. Though less fraught with difficulty and delay, the publishing history of *Old Woman at Play* compares with that of *Crackpot*. In 1978, after Wiseman's unsuccessful attempt to place the book with McClelland and Stewart, Clarke, Irwin undertook to issue *Old Woman at Play*. Despite Clarke, Irwin's resolve to produce a beautiful book suited to its unusual subject, Wiseman again proved to be a demanding author in negotiations with her third Canadian publisher. Although she knew the horrible face of rejection, having suffered several deep blows over *Crackpot*, Wiseman had rallied as the spirited author determined to see her work published well or not at all. *Old Woman at Play* was a work of creative non-fiction, conceived as a celebration of her mother's folk art; the text incorporated full-colour photographs of Chaika Waisman's dolls. Negotiations with Jack McClelland, to whom Wiseman first submitted *Old Woman at Play*, and with John Pearce, editorial director of Clarke, Irwin, were marked by Wiseman's usual vigour. As she had done earlier with *Crackpot*, and despite the prolonged difficulties she had experienced with her second novel, she retained control over publication of her work.

Although reviewers were mixed in their response to her daring second novel, many were prepared to celebrate Wiseman's departure from fiction in *Old Woman at Play*. In fact, reviewers recognized the value and importance of *Old Woman at Play* as an original work that incorporated elements of autobiography, biography, memoir, and creative non-fiction. Today, those same reviewers likely would consider the book an example of life writing—the current generic term was not yet in use in the late 1970s—and would respond favourably to its powerful first-person narrative.[1] Despite the praise of reviewers, readers, unfortunately, were less drawn to the book. By 1978, four years following the appearance of *Crackpot*, Wiseman's audience had come to know her as a writer of fiction, an irony not lost on the author who had struggled so long to find a publisher for her second novel. *Old Woman at Play*, distinguished by Wiseman's rare ability as a writer and an iconoclastic thinker, did not attract the readers it merited.

As early as October 1970, while she was working on *Crackpot*, Wiseman recognized the initial stirring of a separate work that later became *Old Woman at Play*. That month, she visited her alma mater, the University of Manitoba in Winnipeg, where for the first time she presented the *Doll Show,* a celebration of her mother's handmade dolls. A one-woman theatrical piece narrated by Wiseman, the *Doll Show* featured Chaika Waisman's creations, constructed out of fabric, buttons, and household scraps. Wiseman's commentary explained the origin of each doll on display, highlighted its unique attributes, and posited imaginary relationships among selected dolls. From 1973 onward, Wiseman presented the *Doll Show*—transported easily in oversized suitcases—across Canada.

Chaika Waisman's dolls.
(Adele Wiseman fonds, Scott Library, York University)

Wiseman had grown interested in her mother's creative work, begun in earnest after Chaika Waisman had retired from dressmaking. She responded to the dolls as naïve folk art, made out of a natural, playful impulse and designed not "TO LAST,"[2] in the tradition of high art, but to give immediate pleasure to the viewer or recipient. The first *Doll Show* gave Wiseman a welcome opportunity to showcase her mother's work and to share with a receptive audience her tentative ideas on creativity. Later, for the purposes of a "doll book"[3] that, by 1970, already was forming in her mind, Wiseman refined and developed a sophisticated exploration of the creative impulse.

Wiseman was uncertain in her literary footing, however. Confident as a writer of fiction, she intuited that the doll book, shapeless as the project may have been in its formative stages, would require formal experimentation. In addition, if she hoped to commemorate the life of Chaika Waisman, whom she knew primarily as mother, she would need to learn more about Waisman's life. Wiseman decided that a visit to Russia, where her mother was born and raised, was necessary. She was determined to write a textured, nuanced narrative of a difficult and complex life and hoped a reunion with members of her mother's family would provide the context she needed for her project. Hence, in the summer of 1971, Wiseman and her husband Dmitry Stone, with their two-year-old daughter Tamara, travelled to Leningrad to visit her maternal relatives, with whom the family had corresponded sporadically over fifty years.

In *Old Woman at Play*, Wiseman recalls her trip to Russia, where she met three aunts and their two surviving husbands, known previously only through childhood stories: "[S]itting quietly on the benches of a shaded boulevard in the afternoon, we talked, exchanging lives, and gazed at each other and briefly, unforgettably, permanently interlocked worlds. . . . I marvelled at the deep resemblance in the bone between my mother . . . myself and them all."[4] In choosing to write about her mother, Wiseman understood that she would be writing about herself, as well. Moreover, the same moral impulse and abiding interest in family history that drove her novels informed her work on the doll book. She may have been uncertain in her choice of genre, but Wiseman was confident in her voice and subject.

Two early experiences consolidated her commitment to the doll book. The first was her trip to Russia, which heightened Wiseman's sense of urgency about the project and her desire to write a family narrative. The second was another *Doll Show* presented on 13 February 1973 at the University of Western Ontario in London. The success of the *Doll Show* was corroborated by James Reaney, a member of the audience who was a professor of English at Western and a friend of Wiseman. Between 1949 and 1956, Reaney had been a member of the Department of English at the University of Manitoba, where he and Wiseman had met. Wiseman also had befriended Reaney's wife, the poet Colleen Thibaudeau. Having seen the celebration of her mother's work, Reaney encouraged Wiseman to proceed with the larger project of a book and he agreed to write to the Canada Council in support of a grant application she submitted in early 1973. By 26 May 1973, as she awaited the council's decision, Wiseman was "feeling all balls in the air at the moment" and she hoped by the fall "to be able to begin on the doll book."[5]

In early October 1973, Wiseman learned that her application had been successful and that she had been awarded a Canada Council Explorations Grant in the amount of $5500 in support of her proposed book. She meant to begin the exciting but difficult work on the project as soon as possible. As she completed *Crackpot* and *Testimonial Dinner*, which was printed privately in 1978, Wiseman looked forward to "get[ting] on to Mom & the doll book. Wow! Balls in the air!"[6] It took her four years, in fact, to write the book she later titled *Old Woman at Play*.

Wiseman acknowledged that she was a slow writer, but her progress on the doll book was determined in large part by the challenging nature of the project. Shaped by plot and the character of Chaika Waisman, *Old Woman at Play* resembles a novel, a narrative form that Wiseman understood well. As a work of life writing, it also incorporates autobiography and an examination of the creative process. In practice, the blending of narrative elements proved difficult and Wiseman struggled to discover the true form of her work. She also felt the pressure of time. In 1975, Chaika Waisman turned eighty years old and was ill with cancer. Wiseman hoped her mother would live to celebrate the publication of her book.

Wiseman's work on the doll book was interrupted by personal responsibilities—the care of her daughter, for example—and professional duties. In 1975–76, she served as writer-in-residence at the University of Toronto's Massey College, the first of several writer-in-residency positions Wiseman held. The position required her to meet with students and discuss their work. Conscientious and affable, Wiseman encouraged young writers to visit her office and took pleasure in nurturing their literary aspirations. One result, however, of her dedication to students was that she devoted too little time to her writing. In a letter to Margaret Laurence, written from her office at Massey College, Wiseman's frustration was palpable: "If I could only manage to get the doll book done."[7] As soon as the academic year ended, she returned to her work with renewed enthusiasm and a will to complete the project.

By August 1977, one year later, she had finished the book. Still hesitant about the form of the doll book (she described it as "curious"), Wiseman felt she had achieved her purpose in commemorating the life and genius of her mother through an exploration of the creative process. As daughter and as writer, she relished her accomplished memoir of a woman who

> mediates, coaxing and soothing herself and us out of our fear and pain, out of superstitious and superficially aesthetic recoil. She makes, in her creations, bridges to lead us to new territories of the heart, to more generous comprehension, to wholer and more satisfying aesthetic. Each junk and button picture, every little doll is an expression of what it's really like "to be," a submission to, a reconciliation with, an acceptance and a celebration of being.[8]

Chaika Waisman's ingenuous nature is evoked in a singular anecdote Wiseman recalls in her book. When Wiseman is shocked to discover her 1956 Governor General's medal sewn into a collage made by her artist mother, Waisman responds ironically: "Why should it just lie around the house?"[9]

WHEN JACK MCCLELLAND DECIDED against publication of her two plays, *The Lovebound* and *Testimonial Dinner* (Wiseman was impressed by the tactful eloquence of his rejection), he softened the blow with a request to see her next book when it was completed. McClelland hoped to maintain friendly relations with Wiseman and to continue as her publisher. He was soon disappointed.

In August 1977, Wiseman sent McClelland *Old Woman at Play*, as the doll book finally was titled. McClelland had been awaiting the work for some time and he was determined to act quickly. He had known from the start that Wiseman would expect her book to include full-colour photographs. Since she had developed an interplay between her written text and her mother's art, illustrations of Chaika Waisman's dolls were to be an essential element of *Old Woman at Play*. McClelland understood that he would have difficulty convincing Wiseman of the prohibitive cost of publishing an illustrated edition of her work. What he could not have anticipated, however, was his antipathy for the text itself.

On 10 August 1977, McClelland gave Linda McKnight his "personal assessment" of *Old Woman at Play*: "[I]t is a very bad book. At best I find it pretentious, self-indulgent, somewhat amaturish [sic] and in many places downright boring."[10] He asked McKnight to respond to the typescript and to circulate it among several senior editors for further evaluation. As he had done earlier with *Crackpot*, McClelland intended to give Wiseman "a decision within two weeks."[11] Throughout their association as publisher and author, McClelland acted out of respect and concern for Wiseman. He understood, for example, that *Old Woman at Play* was "a very important work to Adele. Her mother means a great deal to her. Everyone in the writing fraternity knows she has been working on the book for a long time."[12] By hastening the process of evaluation, he hoped to forestall the author's anxiety over her work.

By the end of September, however, *Old Woman at Play* was still making the rounds at McClelland and Stewart. With the exception of Jennifer Glossop, who found the book "thoroughly enjoyable"[13] and recommended publication, readers responded negatively to the work. Of several readers who reported on the book—Linda McKnight, Frank Newfeld, and Bob Young were among them—none were more scathing than Anna Porter, who admitted, "Honestly, I don't know what to say. I simply do not think this is a book we could publish successfully. . . . Personally, I think it's absolutely hopeless."[14]

McClelland's unfavourable reaction to *Old Woman at Play* was corroborated by other readers. Clearly, he was faced with a dilemma. As publisher, he was unwilling to alienate a valuable author; moreover, company policy, as he explained to Wiseman, "has been to publish authors, not books and thus to publish unperfect works by an author we have confidence in when and if they are given to us."[15] In a letter dated 11 October 1977, McClelland conceded that Wiseman had given him "the toughest publishing problem"[16] he had ever faced. Out of concern for the author, however, he felt an obligation to outline the difficulties presented by *Old Woman at Play*.

First, the book would be costly to produce. Second, McClelland did not believe that a coffee-table book priced at thirty dollars would attract many purchasers. Finally, and most importantly, he asserted that the work was flawed: "[T]he philosophical discussions were rambling, self-conscious and repetitive—interruptive of the warm portrait of your mother." He worried that "critical reaction . . . may be negative and hurtful, not only to the book but to yourself." Although he had little "right to interfere,"[17] McClelland asked Wiseman to consider revising her work.

In spite of these concerns, McClelland was prepared to publish *Old Woman at Play* "in a conventional 6" x 9" format with a maximum of eight pages of full-colour illustrations, bound as one unit."[18] He also offered to include black and white illustrations throughout the text. He was compelled, however, to comment honestly:

> Okay, Adele, we are prepared to publish. If we do we will give it our best shot. We will do a relatively small edition. We will publish at a moderate price. The fact that we have reservations about the script will not surface. We will support it. That's our obligation to you, but my publishing instinct tells me that you have been too close to the script, too emotionally involved, that the structure is wrong, and that it simply won't work in the way you think it will.[19]

Wiseman politely declined to publish *Old Woman at Play* with McClelland and Stewart. McClelland's letter, in fact, may have had the desired effect on Wiseman. No doubt, McClelland sensed she might respond negatively to a letter in which he was at once critical and conciliatory. His previous knowledge of Wiseman as an author who would not waver in her artistic vision may have shaped McClelland's double-edged response to *Old Woman at Play*. Despite McClelland's unflattering assessment, however, and Wiseman's resolve to withdraw the manuscript, relations between publisher and author remained cordial. Only later, when a misunderstanding arose over *Crackpot*, did McClelland and Wiseman part company.

On 17 May 1978, when she learned from friend and fellow writer Marian Engel—in 1976, on Wiseman's recommendation, McClelland had published Engel's controversial novel *Bear*—that 750 overstock hardcover copies of *Crackpot* were being sold at W.H. Smith bookstores at a reduced price of $1.99, Wiseman threatened McClelland: "[T]his goes beyond mere personal gripe. . . . Unless you inform me shortly that what I have said is factually inaccurate, I will be passing this on to the Writers Union." Wiseman decried McClelland's "hostile behavior" and "callous indifference" and she sought to purchase the remaining hardcover stock of *Crackpot*, "to make up my royalty by doing the selling job you obviously didn't feel up to doing yourself."[20]

Hurt and angered by Wiseman's letter, McClelland retaliated: "If you wish to bring this matter or any other aspect of your dealings with McClelland and Stewart to the attention of The Canadian Writers' Union or press or anyone else, by all means do so."[21] McClelland explained that the remaining hardcover copies of *Crackpot* had been sent to Smith's and were not available to Wiseman. Further, he noted that a paperback issue of *Crackpot* was part of McClelland and Stewart's New Canadian Library series and had been published in 1978 "largely at the instigation"[22] of friends. In fact, writers Margaret Laurence and Alice Munro and York University English professor Clara Thomas had written to McClelland to say that an inexpensive, paperback issue of *Crackpot* was necessary "for study purposes."[23] That Wiseman would ignore his former efforts on her behalf led to McClelland's stinging conclusion, where he revealed his heartfelt dismay:

> I will add to the foregoing something that would have gone unsaid had it not been for the nasty, threatening tone of your letter. Because of my respect for you and your work, we undertook to publish CRACKPOT to the best of our ability . . . I think we did a reasonable job. For the same reason, we made what we considered to be a fair and reasonable proposal on the Doll manuscript [i.e. *Old Woman at Play*]. We came away from that experience with a strong feeling that you knew nothing about book publishing; that you were oblivious to the economic realities;

that you had come to believe that the world owes you
some very extraordinary considerations as an artist. I came
away from that interchange depressed and your recent
letter has done nothing to lessen that depression.[24]

An angry Wiseman retaliated that the world did owe artists "extraordinary consideration."[25] Over the years, she had grown convinced
that she was working against the tide of agents, editors, and publishers.
As a result, she frequently targeted publishers—the same men and
women who might issue her work—as recipients of her ire.

Wiseman would not alter her position on *Crackpot* for the sake of
maintaining a professional relationship with McClelland. Increasingly
independent, she could be difficult and testy, traits that McClelland
had come to know too well. Among her publishers, Jack McClelland
was the lone recipient of Wiseman's virulent anger, an unfortunate
indication of the deep frustration she must have felt at mid-career,
marked by the publication of *Crackpot*, when she no longer enjoyed
the success she had known with *The Sacrifice*.

In 1980, following the death of Chaika Waisman, a compassionate
McClelland initiated a reconciliation with Wiseman. On 23 January,
he wrote to Wiseman to say "how very sorry I was to hear the sad
news about your mother. She was clearly one of a kind, an extraor-
dinarily gifted person. I am only sorry that we weren't able to play a
part in the public recognition of that fact."[26] At times of personal crisis
in the lives of authors, McClelland set aside all resentment and offered
comfort. It was, in fact, McClelland's human touch that continued to
impress and move Wiseman. The sting of anger lingered, however, to
prevent a full rapprochement between publisher and author.

Soon after her rejection of McClelland's offer, and acting on the
advice of fellow writer Jack Ludwig, whom she had known as a youth
in Winnipeg, Wiseman submitted *Old Woman at Play* to a newer

publishing house, Lester and Orpen Dennys. Despite their interest in the book, they too felt it would be an expensive undertaking. A third attempt to place her work with a Canadian publisher did prove successful, however.

McClelland's offer to publish *Old Woman at Play* would not have resulted in the attractive, generously illustrated book Wiseman envisaged for her project. Since her mother's craft of doll making formed the subject of the work, Wiseman was convinced that colour photographs of Chaika Waisman's dolls ought to accompany her text. She understood the book would be expensive to produce; nonetheless, Wiseman hoped to find a publisher willing to launch her costly project.

As she had done often in the past, Wiseman sought the counsel of Margaret Laurence. Laurence read the typescript of *Old Woman at Play* and judged it a moving work, worthy of publication. Following its rejection by Lester and Orpen Dennys, Wiseman briefly considered undertaking publication herself. Feeling "desperate," without "reason to believe the book would ever find a publisher," she and Laurence met "to discuss strategies for raising the money to self-publish."[27] Together they estimated the cost of publication with colour photographs to accompany the text. As they might have anticipated, the projected cost of more than $30,000 was prohibitive. Since it was unlikely that the project would attract financial sponsorship, the author resumed her search for a Canadian publisher.

Wiseman's fortuitous decision to submit her work to Clarke, Irwin was spurred by colleagues Timothy Findley—*The Wars*, Findley's landmark novel, was published by Clarke, Irwin in 1977—and Margaret Laurence. As she had done earlier with *Crackpot*, Laurence facilitated publication of Wiseman's work. In late 1977, when John Pearce, editorial director of Clarke, Irwin, contacted Laurence on an unrelated matter, she recognized an opportunity to promote *Old Woman at Play*. Laurence's description of her friend's project piqued Pearce's interest and he agreed to read Wiseman's typescript. As she would admit later, Wiseman felt "lucky, finally, to find a sympathetic publisher and staff in Bill Clarke and his crew at the old Clarke Irwin."[28]

Along with her typescript, Wiseman brought several of her mother's dolls to the offices of Clarke, Irwin on St. Clair Avenue, conveniently located close to her home in midtown Toronto. Pearce was impressed by Wiseman's textured narrative and Chaika Waisman's striking dolls—"How could you say no to anything after that?"[29]—and, from the start, he endorsed publication of *Old Woman at Play*. He elaborated in 2002: "I was absolutely positive but I immediately understood why others might have said no to it on economic grounds."[30] Although he had known about McClelland and Stewart's earlier rejection of the work on artistic as well as economic grounds, Pearce remained open to Wiseman's vision for the book. Pearce noted that his position as a relative newcomer on the Toronto publishing scene (he had arrived in Canada from Britain in 1976 with no previous knowledge of Wiseman's oeuvre) may have worked in Wiseman's favour: "I wasn't judging *Old Woman at Play* on any preconceived notions of her work. I was judging it on its own."[31]

Pearce recognized *Old Woman at Play* as "something quite unique"[32] and he undertook to publish the work for two compelling reasons. First, in 1977, Clarke, Irwin was building its trade list and Wiseman's name, which formerly had garnered international praise, was a welcome addition to its roster of authors. Further, when he learned that the typescript already had been rejected, Pearce felt it was his "cultural duty—I worried that no one else would publish the book"[33]—to issue a work he believed in so strongly. Pearce's intuitive appreciation of Wiseman's artistic vision and his commitment to her project remain impressive, especially for an editor new to Canadian publishing. The moral impulse Pearce brought to his work soon convinced Wiseman of his integrity: here was an editor who would value the seriousness of her writing.

Pearce was troubled, however, by Wiseman's resistance to editorial suggestion (early in their professional relationship she had declared her unwillingness to undertake much revision) and by the cost associated with publication. Pearce met these challenges with his usual acumen. Immediately, he enlisted the support of Laurence to help smooth the editorial path toward publication, and he set about identifying potential sources of funding.

In Pearce's own report, he required minor revisions to *Old Woman at Play*, in particular "more facts" about Wiseman's mother and "justification for some of the [text's] assertions," but he hoped "to be able to do the book."[34] A second reader also endorsed publication but was "not sure about the aesthetic analyses."[35] Finally, Pearce solicited comments from Laurence, whose ten-page report, dated 10 December 1977, reflected her affinity for, and deep knowledge of, Wiseman's work.

Wiseman had suggested Laurence as a potential reader who would understand and endorse the theoretical underpinnings of *Old Woman at Play*. Although she regularly read her friend's work in progress, Laurence admitted that she felt uneasy in her role as professional reader for Clarke, Irwin, and she wondered whether she was "presumptuous" in adopting "an editorial voice."[36] In spite of her reservations, Laurence's report was exemplary for its careful appreciation of Wiseman's project and its willingness to address specific weaknesses in the text. Laurence admired the "form, 'orchestration' and content"[37] of *Old Woman at Play*, including its exploration of the creative process. She suggested, however, that Wiseman tighten the narrative by eliminating repetition, by simplifying theoretical vocabulary, and by signalling the shift that occurs between Chaika Waisman's use of Yiddish (her native language articulated as fluid English) and her use of English (her adopted language articulated as stilted, uneven prose).

Although he had committed to publishing *Old Woman at Play* and had paid Wiseman a royalty advance of $2000, Pearce would not issue a contract until he had secured external funding for the project. To that end, and to expedite publication, he solicited financial support from several sources: the Samuel and Saidye Bronfman Family Foundation, the National Film Board, the Ontario Crafts Council, and the Government of Canada's Multiculturalism Program. Finally, with the promise of generous assistance from the latter, Clarke, Irwin could issue a contract to publish the book, complete with photographs in colour and black and white by Tom Tsuji. In the interim, despite her earlier protest against editorial intervention, Wiseman heeded Laurence's suggestions and made minor revisions to her text. Revisions were completed by the end of May 1978 and publication was set for that fall.

Pearce understood that the work of editing was intense for Wiseman. As a result, he was careful to avoid requests that might frustrate the author. Their relations remained congenial throughout the publication process, largely due to Pearce's sensitivity to Wiseman and the pleasure he derived from *Old Woman at Play*:

> I loved the book from the start. I'm not sure the manuscript needed much revision. I asked Adele if she might move some things around, if she would expand a few scenes or areas of the book. We did a little bit of juggling. But I wasn't expecting her to revise or rewrite. I don't think there is any editorial intervention that would have made the book any different or any more successful than it was.[38]

Wiseman was fortunate in finding an editor who was committed to the same aesthetic vision she had for her book, where design and content would complement one another.

As McClelland and Stewart had done earlier, having undertaken to evaluate her two plays while *Crackpot* was being prepared for publication, Clarke, Irwin assessed twenty-four of Wiseman's children's stories following its acceptance of *Old Woman at Play*. Over the years, Wiseman had written a number of stories for children, which she always had meant to publish. Although Clarke, Irwin found most of her stories "conventional"[39] and would not issue them, she and Pearce remained on friendly terms.

Despite his enthusiasm, Pearce recognized that *Old Woman at Play* was not destined to become a "big book by publishers' standards; it was domestic and intimate."[40] To enhance its market potential, he obtained blurbs from James Reaney and Margaret Laurence, two early supporters of Wiseman's doll book. For Reaney, the effect of *Old Woman at Play* was "like the Bible sweeping into a room with all its characters turned into dolls." Laurence celebrated Wiseman's portrait of her mother: Waisman "expresses a life-view which is both comic and tragic, . . . deeply compassionate to all creatures great and small."

Prior to publication, Pearce also sought to publicize the work. He offered an excerpt to the Toronto magazine *Saturday Night* (it was declined) and he hoped to interest American and British publishers in *Old Woman at Play*. In June 1978, he wrote to Viking Press in New York and Victor Gollancz in London, Wiseman's earliest publishers, to solicit their interest in her latest work. Pearce noted: "[I]t would be greatly advantageous to add a run for the States [and Britain] to our first printing"[41] of *Old Woman at Play*. Although neither company expressed interest in the work, Pearce remained optimistic and looked forward to publication on 25 November 1978.

Wiseman and her friends also promoted her new work. When James Reaney contacted Keith Turnbull of Toronto's Ne'er Do Well Thespians (NDWT) theatre company to suggest that NDWT host a *Doll*

Show (which Wiseman had been touring since 1973) to launch the book, Reaney could not have anticipated the show's success. At Toronto's Bathurst Street Theatre on 22 October 1978, little more than one month prior to publication of the book, NDWT produced afternoon and evening performances of Wiseman's *Doll Show* (for which Wiseman received a fee of $300). Together, Wiseman, her mother, and her nine-year-old daughter, Tamara—whose own artwork decorated the lobby of the theatre—mounted each show. Wiseman later described the close of the first NDWT performance and the powerful effect of Chaika Waisman's dolls on the audience:

> And then, as has always happened at the *Doll Shows*, in one
> body the audience swarmed forward, and in an instant
> the stage was crowded with people, people surrounding
> mom, people wandering and gazing among the dolls,
> people, male and female, laughing, with gratified expres-
> sions on softened faces. There is something liberating
> about the dolls . . . there was something liberating about
> the occasion.[42]

That copies of *Old Woman at Play* were not available on the day of the performances was unfortunate, but the local success of the *Doll Show* probably generated interest in Wiseman's forthcoming book.

Since the market for so unusual a book was uncertain, Clarke, Irwin proceeded with caution. Three thousand copies were printed and it was priced reasonably at $14.95 for an attractive, hard-cover book. A "handsome, well-produced publication, warm and spirited, full of the author's marvellous wit, insight, and clever prose,"[43] *Old Woman at Play* brought great pleasure to Wiseman, her mother, her friends, and her publisher. Upon receiving her copy, Laurence wrote to congratulate Pearce: "[Y]ou have done the most wonderful design and production job . . . the physical appearance of the book is truly worthy of the text. . . . I'm just so delighted."[44] For her friend, Laurence painted the following on a wooden plaque that would hang in Wiseman's home:

> Hurrah for the Doll Book
> Hurrah for Adele
> Hurray for Dimitri
> Tamara as well
> A great shout of joy
> And a lasting hurrah
> For Chaika, the Bobba,
> *Old Woman at Play*.[45]

Despite the lack of interest from Viking and Gollancz, Pearce remained hopeful that he could sell foreign publishing rights to *Old Woman at Play*. The American writer Tillie Olsen, another close friend of Wiseman, was pressed into service by Pearce: "[A]ny help you can manage will be much appreciated. I'm certainly hoping you can run to a brief letter whose contents we might use in promotion [in the United States]."[46] In fact, following publication, Clarke, Irwin embarked on a protracted and impressive search for a foreign publisher who would disseminate *Old Woman at Play* to a wide audience. Pearce's hopes for the work were twofold: he sought to rediscover an international audience for Wiseman's oeuvre, and he meant to build Clarke, Irwin's reputation as a significant publisher.

Almost one year following publication, author and publisher were feeling frustrated by the lack of foreign interest in the book. By October 1979, Clarke, Irwin had contacted more than sixty publishers in the United States, Britain, and Europe. Most publishers replied negatively; others simply ignored the query. In fact, in their heroic attempt to market the book, Clarke, Irwin faced a particular challenge: how to categorize so eclectic a text. That Wiseman's book eluded strict classification seriously hindered Clarke, Irwin's efforts to place it with foreign publishers. Marketing was difficult in Canada, as well. One bookstore displayed *Old Woman at Play* in its "crafts"[47] section, an extreme example of the general confusion that surrounded the book. Ironically, the originality that had impressed Pearce and had led to publication of *Old Woman at Play* was responsible for the work's struggle to attract foreign interest.

Thus, when the reputable George Braziller, a "feisty, independent, maverick firm"[48] in New York, announced it would like to publish *Old Woman at Play*, Pearce felt the offer, though "not ideal, was manna from heaven."[49] After a year of rejections from foreign companies, Pearce welcomed Braziller's overture to issue Wiseman's work. His positive view of Braziller's offer was not shared by the author, however. In fact, Braziller's intention to issue a small print run and to pay Wiseman a limited royalty of less than ten per cent provoked her ire. She felt Braziller had little regard for her artistic vision and considered his offer a purely business arrangement. Although she wanted her book to reach an American audience, she would not accept an unsatisfactory offer, pressure from Bill Clarke and John Pearce notwithstanding.

Hence, Clarke, Irwin lost a valuable opportunity to establish a small but gratifying presence among American publishers, and Wiseman lost an opportunity to rediscover a broad readership, an especially potent loss for an author who at one time had an international audience. In negotiations with Braziller, Wiseman's stubborn streak held. She would not accept an arrangement that might appear to diminish the status of her work as high art. In refusing to compromise—in this instance, by settling for a small print run and a lesser royalty payment—she was asserting herself as a serious writer and affirming the value of her work, a moral vision that, for better or worse, determined the course of her career.

LIKE *CRACKPOT, OLD WOMAN AT PLAY* never was published in the United States or Britain. Despite Pearce's extraordinary efforts to promote Wiseman and her work, *Old Woman at Play* remained a Canadian book marketed through Canadian bookstores. Unlike *Crackpot*, however, which elicited several negative comments, reviewers were unanimous in their praise for *Old Woman at Play* as an original, "captivating book . . . a genuine creation in itself."[50] They admired the work's generic eclecticism and recognized that it was "about dolls in the way that [Richard Adams's] *Watership Down* was . . . about bunnies" (*Maclean's*).[51] Reviewers applauded Wiseman's foray into non-fiction, her successful melding of folk art, social history, biography, and autobiography with a treatise on creativity, and they were intrigued rather than troubled by a text that sought to unify "content and form" (*London Free Press*).[52]

Although Heather Robertson, writing in the *Globe and Mail*, felt that Wiseman's prose, "sophisticated, cultivated [and] . . . beautiful as it is, . . . acts at times . . . as a frustrating barrier"[53] to Chaika Waisman's voice, she admired the daughter's passionate tribute to her mother. Lynne Van Luven recommended *Old Woman at Play* for its "view of life that stems from within and is not merely the product of a carefully-cultivated set of poses and attitudes" (*Lethbridge Herald*).[54] Wiseman's original work of life-writing was appreciated by reviewers who were engaged by her innovative project, authentic voice, and joyous celebration of the creative spirit. Published and reviewed during the holiday season of 1978, *Old Woman at Play* was read as a "healing" book (*Ottawa Journal*).[55]

Readers, however, dissuaded perhaps by both price and genre, were less interested in Wiseman's latest book. Sales of *Old Woman at Play* were too modest to warrant a reprinting for the Canadian market. In addition, Clarke, Irwin's financial difficulties, which by 1980 were considerable, may have contributed to the eventual disappearance of the book. In 1983, in the midst of an economic recession, the fifty-three-year-old Clarke, Irwin went into receivership and Wiseman's hopes for a reprinting were defeated. No doubt, she would have been heartened by an event that took place late that year. On 23 October 1983, producer Howard Rypp of Nephesh Theatre launched a half-hour videofilm of *Old Woman at Play* at Habourfront's Studio Theatre in Toronto.[56]

Today, *Old Woman at Play* remains out of print, accessible only in libraries and rare book shops. As Pearce explained:

> Although the book was not in trouble from the start, there were a lot of things stacked against it. *Old Woman at Play* was surprisingly avant-garde, much less linear, much more complex than most books of its time. Plus the whole question of category affected its sales. There were many people who thought it was neither fish nor fowl; they did not quite know what it was.[57]

She may have felt dejected by the lack of interest in her work, but Wiseman questioned neither the integrity and importance of *Old Woman at Play*, nor her rejection of George Braziller's offer to publish the book in the United States. That Bill Clarke and John Pearce did not sever ties with Wiseman over that rejection confirms their regard for the author and their commitment to her work. Early in their relationship, Pearce recognized and accepted Wiseman's independent nature. He remained an ally and, had Clarke, Irwin survived, he would have been pleased to publish Wiseman's subsequent work. That privilege was given next, however, to Richard Teleky, acquisitions editor at Oxford University Press, who commissioned *Memoirs of a Book Molesting Childhood and Other Essays*, Wiseman's volume of essays published in 1987.

RICHARD TELEKY WAS HIRED BY OXFORD in 1976 and rose to the position of managing editor. Born in Cleveland, Ohio, Teleky immigrated to Canada in 1968 in protest against the Vietnam War. After completing his doctoral studies in English at the University of Toronto, he taught for three years at Toronto's York University before embarking on a career in publishing. Teleky met Wiseman in the early 1980s and they developed a friendship. Early in 1985, when he and Wiseman started "talking about the essay book, . . . she wasn't producing a lot but she was interested in thinking about her past."[58] Having conceived the Oxford series Studies in Canadian Literature, Teleky asked if Wiseman would like to participate in the project. As editor, he was "interested in ethnicity as it touches on literature,"[59] and he grew convinced that Wiseman ought to have a book in the series. Teleky hoped to renew public interest in her work and believed that a collection of essays by Wiseman would attract attention, since she had not published anything in that genre. Wiseman accepted his offer, received a royalty advance of $3000, and in December 1985 submitted a first set of essays, gathered from material she had on hand.

Although Oxford had intended to publish the book in 1986, its deadline proved flexible. In 1986–87, Wiseman was writer-in-residence at the University of Western Ontario and her work on the manuscript was slow. Teleky urged Wiseman to write more "memoir-type essays" and admitted that "it took a long time of working with her to get the final manuscript."[60] Although several of the essays had been published previously,[61] Wiseman felt hesitant about the venture. The essay was a new form for her and she struggled to produce a strong volume. Nonetheless, as she had done with previous editors, Wiseman explained at the beginning of the project "that she did not like editing and would stand by every bit of punctuation."[62] Undaunted, Teleky saw that she "needed someone to ask questions so I edited her in advance of the writing."[63] In practice, Teleky's method of unobtrusive editing facilitated Wiseman's writing and by the close of August 1987 she had completed work on the manuscript.

Although he felt that a number of essays could use further editing, such as Wiseman's study of Henry James's *The Portrait of a Lady*,[64] Teleky let the work go to press. Oxford University Press held world rights to *Memoirs of a Book Molesting Childhood*, which was priced at $13.95. Upon publication, several reviewers noted the uneven quality of the essays. Most, however, like Ken Adachi, appreciated a collection that "proceeds by accumulation of perceptions, making connections and discoveries, occasionally pausing like a connoisseur to admire a cadence or point up a metaphor" (*Toronto Star*).[65] Elizabeth Greene celebrated Wiseman's essays as "associative, complex; they dart back and forth in time and tone and resist a simple schematization" (*Whig-Standard Magazine*),[66] and Sharon Drache enjoyed their "sense of mad celebration" (*Ottawa Jewish Bulletin and Review*).[67]

The writer's persona, "serious, sincere almost to a fault, unironical, loyal and sentimental,"[68] charmed most reviewers, none more than Glen Deer, however, who lauded her "ebullient and colourful confidence about sexuality, political life, and the morality of literature. Wiseman has the ability, rare in any writer, both to tell us what it feels like to be gripped by the pleasures of the book and to engage us in her passionately moral vision of literature's purpose" (*Canadian Literature*).[69] Like her fiction, Wiseman's essays were illuminating. As Marion K. Quednau affirmed, the best moments in *Memoirs of a Book Molesting Childhood and Other Essays* "rely on that accident of truth which seems to sneak up" on a writer "almost unnoticed" (*Globe and Mail*).[70] In 1988, Wiseman received the Montreal Jewish Public Library's J.I. Segal Foundation Award for her collection of essays.

In persuading Wiseman to produce a volume of essays, Teleky had hoped to "kick-start"[71] her career, which had lain dormant since 1978, following the appearance of *Old Woman at Play*. He suggested, for example, that she also prepare a collection of stories and felt certain that had she had more time (between 1983 and 1991, Wiseman worked unstintingly as writer-in-residence at several universities) and "had she not been ill with sarcoma those last few years, she might have persisted more around a short story collection."[72] Wiseman's professional relationship with Teleky extended to his own work. She encouraged his writing of short fiction and did not treat him as a "journeyman writer."[73] Teleky regarded Wiseman as a mentor and appreciated the lack of pretense and honesty in her writing.

Teleky enjoyed Wiseman's dynamic personality as much as he valued her writing: "She was warm and opinionated, not afraid to say what she thought. She was not destructive when she didn't like something or someone's work. She was generous but not a fool. She was not learned in any way; her taste was sometimes eccentric and it could even be coloured by affection. I admired all that."[74] Their lasting connection, founded on friendship and mutual regard, extended to their shared enjoyment of lentil soup—prepared lovingly for Wiseman and delivered by a concerned Teleky during the author's final illness.

THE WRITING AND PUBLICATION of *Old Woman at Play* marked a permanent shift in Wiseman's career away from fiction, which in 1956 had established her reputation as a writer of international stature, to non-fiction and poetry, the latter largely unpublished. Wiseman valued the encouragement and foresight of editors John Pearce and Richard Teleky, who recognized the enduring value of her personal narrative and, against all odds, undertook to publish *Old Woman at Play* and

Memoirs of a Book Molesting Childhood and Other Essays. In a late interview published in 1987, however, Wiseman scorned publishing practice:

> It works this way. You write a book and it is published. If you want to be in what is called the big time, you should immediately follow up with another book with the same general ideas as the first one, a kind of sequel. *The Sacrifice* had three big-name publishers, Macmillan, Viking, and Gollancz, but I didn't produce the same mode of writing again. That simply wasn't my intention, and they weren't interested.[75]

Although her evaluation of publishing practice is accurate, Wiseman's comment is valuable more for what it reveals of the aging author: the disappointment she felt in late career and her willingness to dismiss the extraordinary support she had received from editors and publishers over the years.

From the start, Wiseman was determined to chart the course of her career and she often was frustrated when publishers would not accede to her direction. Nonetheless, her wilful, iconoclastic personality frequently won her friends among editors and publishers. Her success, in fact, had much to do with the early triumph of *The Sacrifice* and the regard it engendered for its young author, who grew confident in her talent and certain of her artistic vision. As we have seen, Wiseman's confidence was nurtured first by Robert Weaver, Kildare Dobbs, John Morgan Gray, Marshall Ayres Best, and Victor Gollancz; it was encouraged later by Jack McClelland, John Pearce, and Richard Teleky. In truth, there was much to celebrate in Wiseman's professional relationships. In spite of difficulties that erupted and later subsided, good will was shared among Wiseman, her editors, and publishers, each of whom sought to advance her writing and her career.

FOUR

Years of Mentorship

FOLLOWING THE PUBLICATION OF OLD WOMAN AT PLAY, Wiseman devoted less time to her own writing and focussed on her work as mentor to other writers. By 1979, Dmitry Stone had left Beak Consultants and was self-employed as a consulting biologist. Until their divorce in 1990, Wiseman's mentoring work, especially as writer-in-residence at several Canadian universities, augmented Stone's income and helped support her family.

Temperamentally suited to assisting others, Wiseman learned to value the experience of mentorship. As a young writer, she had the fortunate experience of fruitful mentorship. As we have seen, she was an undergraduate student of Malcolm Ross, who urged her to expand and develop a short story published later as *The Sacrifice*, Wiseman's mature first novel. The writing of that novel also was aided by the regular counsel and advice of Margaret and William Stobie. Moreover, Adele Wiseman and Margaret Laurence met as fledgling writers and developed an enduring friendship and a bond of mentorship. Over forty years, they read and responded to one another's work.

Later, Wiseman's literary community expanded to include writers from around the globe, many of whom were women, who provided encouragement to one another, often across considerable distances. Wiseman's positive experiences as protege informed her professional work as mentor to countless writers. In fact, the view of herself as accomplished derived not only from her writerly successes but from her ability to build mentoring relationships with other writers.

David Lazar writes in his essay "On Mentorship" that "[t]he classic mentor narrative is hierarchical. This, as should be obvious, is a masculine narrative."[1] Wiseman did much to challenge the hierarchical and masculine model of mentorship. In her several capacities as professor of English at Macdonald College of McGill University, as manuscript assessor for the Canada Council, as freelance reviewer, as writer-in-residence at several universities, as director of the May Writing Studios at the Banff Centre for the Arts, and as an accessible and available senior writer, Wiseman nurtured and supported aspiring writers.

The experience of mentorship, often at the centre of a writer's life, has been all but ignored by literary scholarship, which focusses primarily on textual and critical concerns. Lazar goes on to explain:

> Mentorship as a topic for literary discussion is, surprisingly, somewhat rare. Partially, no doubt, because it intrudes on the Promethean myth of creativity. What Creator needs a boost over the wire fence of ignorance, of political, logistical or neurotic obstacles? To discuss the mentor relationship center-stage may invoke feelings—to invoke another myth—that one's rugged individualism is neither so rugged, nor so individual.[2]

As Elizabeth Meese argues, however, to properly "appraise women's contributions to literary culture," critics must seek "a fuller

Adele Wiseman and
Margaret Laurence,
Sunday, 5 October 1986
at Laurence's home,
8 Regent Street, Lakefield,
Ontario. This is the last
photograph of Wiseman
and Laurence together.
(Adele Wiseman fonds, Scott
Library, York University)

understanding of literary roles other than authorship."[3] Wiseman
scholars know, in fact, that her "contributions to the Canadian literary community cannot be measured only in terms of publications."[4]
Mentorship, frequently dismissed as a means of supplementing a
writer's income and secondary to the work of writing, helped shape
Wiseman's career and allowed her to influence the literary careers of
other writers. Moreover, Wiseman's valuing of a community of writers
that supported a shared desire to make art was given unique expression
in her work as mentor. Mentorship was an important creative outlet
for Wiseman that also served the needs of her students, colleagues, and
peers. As writer Sylvia Fraser recognized, "Adele became muse and
advocate for several generations of artists."[5]

Wiseman's experience as mentor confirms Lazar's view that "[r]ecently . . . other models, other stories [of mentorship] have emerged, in part because of the emergence of women's stories of mentorship."[6] Her career as mentor formally began in September 1963 with her appointment to the position of lecturer (later assistant professor) in the Department of English, Macdonald College of McGill University, where she taught first-year agriculture students. That same year (1963–64), she was adjunct professor in the Department of English at Sir George Williams (now Concordia) University. Previously, Wiseman had taught English to grade five students at the Overseas School of Rome and had tutored in the Department of English at the University of Manitoba, but in both positions she was still an apprentice writer. By 1963, at the age of thirty-five, she had completed her education; she had lived for extended periods in London, Rome, and New York, and had travelled to Hong Kong; she had published her first novel, had completed a second project, her play *The Lovebound*, and had begun preliminary work on her second novel; she had attended Yaddo and MacDowell writers' colonies; and she had received several important awards, including a Governor General's Award and a Guggenheim Fellowship. The faculty appointment at Macdonald College consolidated Wiseman's connection with the university that continued throughout her life in various capacities at a number of Canadian institutions.

Unfortunately, little record remains of Wiseman's academic career. Conscientiously well prepared, she was wide-ranging in her lectures and urged students to be honest in their writing as a way of cultivating a distinctive style. No doubt, she stimulated her students as she later inspired young writers in her capacity as writer-in-residence and through her work at the Banff Centre for the Arts. Certainly, Wiseman would have brought her incisive intelligence, generous spirit, and warm sense of humour—personality traits that have been celebrated by many—to undergraduate teaching.

Wiseman's move to the greater Toronto area in 1969 precipitated her decision to devote her time to writing and to raising her daughter. As a professional, however, she sought to strengthen her ties with the literary community in Canada. What followed were years of mentorship that called upon her rare ability to assist those who solicited her expert skill.

Wiseman soon became a manuscript assessor for the Writing and Publishing Section of the Canada Council (under the direction of Naim Kattan), freelance work she continued between 1970 and 1990. During this time, she also resumed book reviewing, which she had begun during her stay in London in the 1950s. Then she had reviewed works for the *Jewish Quarterly* and the *Jewish Chronicle*. Now, however, Wiseman turned her attention to works of fiction and non-fiction by Canadian writers and wrote for Canadian journals and newspapers, including *Books in Canada* and the *Toronto Star*.

As manuscript assessor and book reviewer, Wiseman worked to enhance and promote literary culture in Canada. She gave every project, large and small, serious consideration and understood that her assessments would assist the development of writers. The manuscripts received from the Canada Council she read closely and carefully, and she took similar care with her published reviews. Her evaluations of the work of other writers were fair and insightful and refused obdurate criticism. Wiseman's character as facilitating mentor was felt in reviews that proposed to elucidate a work and engage the reader. She eschewed the posture of condemning critic who, in reviewing, aimed to reveal her egoistic self rather than serve the interests of the writer and the work under consideration.

Wiseman celebrated the disturbing over the familiar. In her review of Marian Engel's intriguing novel *Bear*, for example, she noted with characteristic aplomb: "[I]f we were to limit ourselves to what the nice people of the world at any given time find immediately acceptable, we would have no literature. The alarm bells of the present ring in the insights of the future."[7] She also admired Margaret Atwood's "sense of mischief" in *Life before Man*: "Atwood's is an imagination with a long reach, and the ingenuity to avoid being caught reaching."[8] Myrna Kostash, author of *All of Baba's Children*, "is a scrapper, and the pain of the sacrificial generations [of Ukrainian immigrants to Canada] is in her, as is the injured pride of the implied inheritance of second-class citizenship."[9] Helen Weinzweig was praised for "her experimentation with fluid and shifting psychic states"[10] in *Basic Black with Pearls*, as was Sylvia Fraser for articulating "the failure of the beautiful, the lucky, the rich and the gifted . . . to shoulder the responsibilities that luck and gifts imply."[11]

Wiseman's work and reputation (by 1974 she had published her second novel) continued to bring her into contact with other writers. Sylvia Fraser, seven years her junior, remembers:

> My benefits of friendship with Adele were always far more obvious than hers with me: she became my literary mentor—no honorary appointment. Over the years, she cheerfully read a series of desperate and groping manu-scripts served up in plastic grocery bags, supremely un-daunted by chapters that rolled over and died or else took off in several directions at once, able to see far better than I where all this compulsive typing could be leading. Adele's criticisms, tactfully delivered over soup and deli food in her cluttered kitchen, were pithy rather than detailed.[12]

Poet and teacher Kenneth Sherman described meeting Wiseman soon after he published his review of *Crackpot*[13] and the sage advice she offered him: "Work to support your family while you work at becoming a writer."[14] In her memorial poem "The Hooded Hawk,"

Anne Michaels recalls that Wiseman's "face had the tenderness / of a hand."[15]

Frequently, younger writers felt a connection with Wiseman through her work. Poet Janis Rapoport, for example, recognized Wiseman as mentor "through her books, through knowing her as the person who wrote those books and created those characters with such insight,"[16] and novelist Sharon Drache felt inspired especially by *The Sacrifice*.[17] In person and through her writing, Wiseman was a mentor who "cast light and shadow, complicate[d] the foreground. . . . reveal[ed] for a time" what she could.[18] Wiseman's presence, like that of her own mentors, often could be felt "in the margins"[19] of another writer's work. Over the years, the many letters of reference Wiseman wrote in support of job and grant applications provided further assistance to writers.

As we have already seen, two mentorships resulted in publication. Wiseman helped mend a rift between publisher Jack McClelland and her friend and fellow writer Marian Engel, leading to the 1976 publication of Engel's *Bear*. In 1975, soon after McClelland had published *Crackpot*, Wiseman urged Engel's "fine serious fiction" on her publisher:

> Briefly, it's the story of a physical relationship which a lady has with a bear; I state that baldly to get it over with, because that, though crucial, is only the concrete vehicle, and a damn good one at that. What is, from my point of view, so fascinating about this book is that she's really saying something that goes beyond the apparent "grossness" of some of the action, something which manages, in fact, to reconcile us to it . . . Of course the physical stuff will provide the public furor and delectation which I've suggested above, but you will see for yourself that it

actually evolves as an absolute, inevitable necessity of a beautifully controlled, balanced narrative.

Knowing that McClelland would appreciate her foresight in bringing *Bear* to his attention, Wiseman signed herself his "little literary Goody Two Shoes."[20] In fact, McClelland embraced the originality of Engel's fiction and his offer to publish her award-winning novel (*Bear* won the Governor General's Award in 1976) ended a quarrel that had divided publisher and author for a number of years. Wiseman's mentoring strategy resembled that of Margaret Laurence, who, as we already know, drew on professional connections to facilitate publication of a friend's work.

Editor Richard Teleky and Wiseman developed a mentoring friendship rooted in a shared artistic sensibility. As acquisitions editor at Oxford University Press, Teleky suggested that Wiseman gather her essays and revise them as *Memoirs of a Book Molesting Childhood and Other Essays*. Had it not been for Teleky's editorial vision, Wiseman's essays likely would not have been issued as a single volume. An aspiring writer himself, Teleky appreciated Wiseman's generous counsel and reciprocal reading of his own early fiction.

Opportunities for mentorship expanded during the 1970s and 1980s when Wiseman regularly gave presentations on literature and participated in literary conferences. In July 1981, for example, along with Gary Geddes, Geoff Hancock, Robert Kroetsch, Patrick Lane, Alice Munro, and Suzanne Paradis, Wiseman was invited by the Chinese Writers' Association to visit China for twelve days as Canada's unofficial literary ambassadors. "[D]etermined to make this cultural exchange as real a dialogue as possible," the group of writers traversed a vast cultural divide and successfully "represent[ed] our country and professions."[21] They spent their time sightseeing, promoting the work of Canadian authors, and meeting with Chinese writers, and soon discovered that mutual understanding was founded on a willingness "to face each other in our own contexts."[22]

Between 1975 and 1991, Wiseman held writer-in-residency positions at several Canadian universities, including Massey College, University of Toronto (1975–76); Trent University (24–28 January 1983); Concordia University (1983–84); the University of Western Ontario (1986–87); the University of Prince Edward Island (fall 1987); and three years at the University of Windsor (1988 to 1991). Wiseman "set out from the start to make sure she was approached and approachable."[23] Phyllis Grosskurth, emeritus professor of English at the University of Toronto, confirmed Wiseman's important influence and remarkable willingness to counsel students during her year as writer-in-residence at Massey College,[24] for example. In her first week at the University of Toronto, an advertisement in the *Varsity*, a campus newspaper, announced her office hours: "9–3 Tuesday, Wednesday, Thursday."[25]

A self-described "enabler," Wiseman sought to help students "see more clearly where they are going."[26] She was indefatigable, available for consultation and serious in her approach to students, careful not to trod on aspiring writers. Conscious of personal bias, she admitted, "There are so many different kinds of writing these days that I couldn't presume to tell someone whether they'll ever be good or not. Someone could be very good at a type of writing that I wouldn't particularly want to read."[27] Officemate Lenore Langs recalled that

> Adele did a great deal for the craft of writing and for writers while she was at the University of Windsor, but . . . her greatest achievement was that she created an environment wherein artists from many different disciplines—music, drama, literature, visual arts—were able to come together to work for the enrichment of all.[28]

The final position Wiseman held before her death, as Head of the May Writing Studios at the Banff Centre for the Arts, was one she appreciated. The Banff appointment, cut short by her death in 1992, might have marked the beginning of a new stage in Wiseman's career when her work as mentor would become more formalized. As Ingrid MacDonald notes, "Banff gave her a place not only to be a writer, but to extend to other writers a utopian opportunity: to be a writer, to be fed, housed, given community and respect."[29] As a place where artists, and especially writers, felt valued for the important and challenging work they undertook, Banff articulated an ideal for Wiseman and provided the freedom to exercise her gift for inspiring others. Don Coles acknowledged that Wiseman "ran the program with a passion . . . that lifted and energized everyone who came near her."[30] Amid the atmosphere and setting of Banff, Wiseman excelled as mentor, as several participants later testified.

Caroline Adderson, for example, was convinced of Wiseman's "superior gifts . . . we had her writing, but also her loyalty, her mother-knows-best, her fearless muscling around."[31] Stella Body soon saw "that Adele's presence, off-kilter as it always is with convention, even with the ordinary laws of conversation, is as charged with meaning for others in the group as it is for me."[32] Body and other participants also were impressed by Wiseman's "fierceness, her mental courage. . . . she fights tirelessly in the battle for freedom of the mind."[33] Wiseman encouraged a sense of community and would concede little difference between novice and established writers: "[I]t was as tough for her as it was for us."[34]

As "materfamilias"[35] at Banff, Wiseman "set a high standard of honesty and integrity";[36] at the same time, she intuited the needs of writers and sought to direct them toward their goals. Whether present or not—in her latter two years as Head of the May Writing Studios, Wiseman was ill from complications related to sarcoma and not always on-site—her generous spirit and "shining energy"[37] remained palpable. Ven Begamudré recalled the power of Wiseman's influence: "[E]ven in Adele's absence, the program was still hers."[38]

Wiseman's unusual success as mentor lay not so much in the practical counsel she gave students and aspiring writers, familiar advice that emphasized the importance of reading, of paying attention to the uses of language, and the value of revision.[39] Nor did it reside entirely in her passionate "word-wizard[ry],"[40] her whirling of words "like tossed firecrackers, words no one else uses: *shibboleth, flapdoodle, prolixity.*"[41] Rather, Wiseman's genius as mentor was rooted in an uncanny ability to "read from people's eyes where their thoughts will move, and pursue them there, with a quickness of lightning."[42] As "someone who barely knew" Wiseman, Elizabeth Greene admitted that "she made a great difference to me. . . . [She had] a gift of vision and belief that helped friends, fellow writers and students"[43] achieve their goals.

There is no doubt that Wiseman's published work continues to have a profound effect on readers and writers. Wiseman's legacy as mentor, a legacy she nurtured throughout her professional life, is more difficult to establish, however, since the record of effective mentorship invariably is embedded in the idiosyncratic exchanges of protege and mentor. As Lazar suggests, however, "[t]he desire for direction, for wisdom, precisely when we have, with so much resistance, uncovered the Achilles heel of authority, uncovers new possibilities for mentoring, and puts us at an initiate's disadvantage when we act like tyromaniacs, shooting down the authority we seek."[44] Wiseman herself eschewed the authority of the "classic mentor narrative."[45] Perhaps her example of mentorship, radical in its unprepossessing design and natural delivery, shaped by intuition and common sense, offered the authority and guidance most appreciated by novice and practiced writers alike.

IN HER MEMORIAL TRIBUTE to Marian Engel, a dear friend and fellow writer, Wiseman revealed much of herself:

> Though the death of Marian Engel, on 16 February 1985, after a long struggle with cancer, was not totally unexpected, it was felt in the literary community like a sudden withdrawal of current, a dimming of lights. This consciousness of the loss of a distinct vitality is still with us. Marian did not go gently. There was no folding up of tents here, but rather the feisty determination to be taken, if at all, in midsentence, to leave her voice still ringing. She has left those of us who knew her and respected her work with a continuing regret for a life too early, a unique voice too soon interrupted.[46]

Wiseman's words echo across her own life and death. She herself showed a "feisty determination"; she refused to submit to the judgement of others and was committed to the "ringing" cadence of her own voice. She, too, died "after a long struggle," with sarcoma, on 1 June 1992 at the age of sixty-four, and experienced the frustration of being taken "too early," before the completion of her life's work.

Wiseman's death elicited an outpouring of words that testified to the lasting impact of her life and work. Obituaries recorded her achievement as writer and mentor—Wiseman sought to "shape life so that it becomes favorable to art"[47]—and the extent to which she touched others: "Even during the period of her last illness, she never hesitated to offer advice—whether personal or professional—to the many friends who came by to see her."[48] A memorial tribute on 24 June 1992 at Toronto's Factory Theatre brought together Wiseman's family members, friends, and fellow writers, many of whom appear in the pages of this book.[49] That Toronto's Factory Theatre was full to capacity affirmed Wiseman's abiding connection with her audience, despite the vagaries of her career. Indeed, Wiseman was fortunate in her ability to reach readers and in her literary connections. Readers benefited from her insight; literary friends from her ability to inspire their best work. As poet Linda Rogers commented in 1999, Wiseman "had enough soul for a full-figured gospel choir."[50]

Following her first brilliant success with *The Sacrifice*, Wiseman's attempts to write of "truth and understanding and love"[51] did not always reach the metaphoric heights of the choir loft, however. Unwilling to concede to market conditions that called for a second novel, Wiseman turned her attention to drama. By the time *The Lovebound* was completed and had made the rounds of editors and publishers, finally to languish unproduced and unpublished, years had lapsed, the reading public's attention had been forfeited, and Wiseman's currency as the author of *The Sacrifice* had diminished significantly. Moreover, when *Crackpot* finally was issued, Wiseman faced the difficult challenge of regaining an audience after a publishing hiatus of eighteen years. That she had created an unusually convincing protagonist in Hoda secured her place as a strong novelist, but she would go on to write from the margins, without the wide readership she enjoyed as a younger writer.

Always the agent at the centre of her career, however, Wiseman did not regard her incremental loss of literary recognition as fatal. Her monumental success as a first-time novelist, when she won prestigious awards and honours and reached an international audience, did not impede her vision of the writer as moral witness to her time. In fact, as Wiseman's career unfolded with increasing difficulty, she grew convinced of the integrity of her vision of the writer. The further away she moved from the exhilarating success of *The Sacrifice*, the more she believed that her work held meaning outside market conditions, that her conditions for writing—of "truth and understanding and love"[52]—existed outside the arena of awards and prizes that marked her early career. Despite her triumphs and disappointments, Wiseman celebrated her place in the literary field as an author for whom the moral imperatives of writing always superceded the economic imperatives of publishing practice. She asserted her artistic agency among literary agents, editors, and publishers and charted the course of her literary path, however many turns and obstacles it presented.

Wiseman's writing endures and her more challenging work is now held in esteem. *Crackpot*, for example, is regarded today as an "unsung"[53] Canadian classic, "perhaps one of the finest novels written in the English language"; it is "hard to imagine another character as brilliantly conceived as Hoda, the humanist hooker"[54] as protagonist. In 1993, critic Laura McLauchlan recognized that *Old Woman at Play* may "have been almost too original"[55] when it was published in 1978. Also in 1993, critic Donna Bennett understood that

> Wiseman's essays repeated her method of understanding and of living in the world, which is to reject facts when necessary, examine context, and test against one's own experience those ideas that appear to explain experience. Then she would have us see new experiences in light of what we remember, and recognize truth when it shines forth.[56]

Wiseman's earliest work, *The Sacrifice*, remains a profound novel of "compassion"[57] by a gifted writer. As renowned book reviewer Robert Adams declared on 30 March 1993, less than one year following her death, Wiseman's "unique achievement" was to "look at a single moment in a human life and see in it the universality of the human condition with all its pain and its mystery."[58]

In Wiseman's career there was much to celebrate and much to regret, not least the inability to complete a third novel that tantalized her in later years. In "That Third Big Fiction," poet and friend Seymour Mayne evokes Wiseman's final, unwritten work that

> gnawed,
> held you like a crab
> in the pincer
> grip of its claw
> and then worked its way
> deeper[59]

Had she been given more time, she may have been "able to pull that novel from the teeth of the ultimate brute. And then why not another?"[60] Ever feisty and determined to chart her own course, even in her final illness, Wiseman looked to the future and dreamed of possibilities for her writing, perhaps one last work of fiction that would unfold "like a passion, impelling the reader along the driving, perfectly focused, obsessively single-minded arc of its action. . . . [leaving] one a little shocked, a little shaken, and, if one can bring oneself to relinquish the safety of familiar absolutes, more than a little enriched."[61] Ample evidence of Wiseman's belief in the transformative potential of the writer's work lies in the lasting quality of her own creative achievement, an achievement recognized by the editors and publishers, mentors and proteges, family members and friends who supported her throughout her career and celebrated her triumphs.

Adele Wiseman: A Chronology

21 May 1928 Born to Chaika (née Rosenberg) and Pesach Waisman (later Wiseman) of Winnipeg, Manitoba. Third of four children: Miriam, Harry, Adele, Morris. The family lives behind her parents' tailoring shop.

1932 Family moves to 490 Burrows Avenue, their permanent residence in Winnipeg's North End.

Attends I.L. Peretz School; Liberty Temple School; Luxton School; Machray School; William White School, Winnipeg.

1944 Grade 11, Junior Matriculation, St. John's Technical High School, Winnipeg. Second prize, short story contest in *Torch*, St. John's Technical High School.

1945 Grade 12, Senior Matriculation, St. John's Technical High School.

Summer 1945–48 Supervisor, Norquay Park Kiddie Playground, Public Parks Board; salesperson; printing-plant worker, Winnipeg.

1946 Sellers Scholarship in Arts; Delta Phi Epsilon Bursary, University of Manitoba, Winnipeg.

Summer 1947 Margaret and Jack Laurence move to Burrows Avenue opposite the Wisemans' home.

28 June–13 Sept. 1947 Guest columnist, "Fanfare" (Roland Penner's entertainment column) *Westerner: Truth and Justice for the West*.

1947–48 Enrols in Malcolm Ross's seminar, "English Thought in the Seventeenth Century." Ross encourages Wiseman to develop a short story into her novel, *The Sacrifice*.

1948–49 Tutor and essay marker, Department of English, University of Manitoba.

1949 Honours BA, English (major) and Psychology (minor), University of Manitoba.

Chancellor's Prize for "Nor Youth Nor Age," short story in *Creative Campus: Literature and Arts* (Spring 1950), University of Manitoba.

Sept. 1950 Accepted by Graduate College, State University of Iowa, for advanced study in creative writing. Wiseman declines offer.

Aug. 1950–July 1951 Resident worker, Stepney Jewish Girls' (B'nai B'rith) Club and Settlement, London, England. Student Club leader for children ages five to fourteen. Edits newsletter, *Stepney Jester*. Writes *The Sacrifice*.

Aug. 1951–June 1952 Teacher (grade five), Overseas School of Rome, Italy.

Summer 1952 Vice-Superintendent, Summer School Camp, Overseas School of Rome. Completes first draft of *The Sacrifice*.

Fall 1952–Apr. 1955 Tutor and essay marker, Department of English, University of Manitoba.

1953 Technical assistant, Dominion Food Pests Entomological Laboratory, Winnipeg.

1954–30 Apr. 1955 Executive secretary, Royal Winnipeg Ballet, Winnipeg.

28–31 July 1955 Attends Canadian Writers' Conference, Queen's University, Kingston, Ontario: "The Writer, His Media, and the Public."

Aug.–Oct. 1955 Apt. 2, 1241 St. Mark Street, Montreal, Quebec. Stays with her elder sister, Miriam.

Oct. 1955–Nov. 1957 16 Barwell House, Cheshire Street, Bethnal Green, London, England. Revises *The Sacrifice* while working again at Stepney. Edits *Stepney Jester* (July 1956).

27 Oct. 1955 Viking Press of New York offers to publish *The Sacrifice*. (Viking contract is signed on 9 November 1955; Wiseman receives a royalty advance of $1000US.) When this offer is finalized, the Macmillan Company of Canada offers to publish the novel as well. (Macmillan contract is signed on 2 February 1956; Wiseman receives a royalty advance of $300Cdn.)

8 Nov. 1955 Margaret Stobie reads an excerpt from *The Sacrifice* on *Anthology*, CBC Radio.

22 Mar. 1956 Victor Gollancz of London, England, offers to publish *The Sacrifice*. (Gollancz contract is signed on 29 March 1956; Wiseman receives a royalty advance of £150.)

May 1956 Trip to Italy.

13 Sept. 1956 *The Sacrifice* is published simultaneously in New York and Toronto; London publication follows on 22 October 1956.

1956 Governor General's Literary Award for fiction.

1957 National Conference of Christians and Jews Brotherhood Award; Beta Sigma Phi Sorority Award.

14 Jan. 1957 Signs contract with Rizzoli Editore for Italian edition of *The Sacrifice*. Receives a royalty advance of £91 13s.

20 Feb. 1957 Signs contract with H. Nelissen for Dutch edition of *The Sacrifice*. Receives a royalty advance of £50.

June–July 1957 Trip to Montreal, Winnipeg, and New York. Attends Canadian Authors' Association Convention in Winnipeg. Receives Governor General's Award and Beta Sigma Phi Sorority Award at Winnipeg celebrations.

Nov. 1957–Jan. 1960 Apt. 12C, 310 West End Avenue, New York. Stays with her friend, British photographer Amy Zahl. Lives on a Canada Foundation Fellowship in creative writing (May 1957 to April 1958; $2700) and a Guggenheim Fellowship (May 1958 to 15 May 1959; $3000US). Writes *The Lovebound: A Tragi-Comedy.*

2 Oct.–2 Dec. 1958 Yaddo writers' colony, Saratoga Springs, New York.

Sept.–Nov. 1959 Trip to Winnipeg.

Oct. 1959–Apr. 1960 Scholarship, Canada Council ($1000 plus travel).

c1960 *The Lovebound: A Tragi-Comedy* (two-act play), is printed privately for the author.

5 Jan.–5 Mar. 1960 Yaddo writers' colony, Saratoga Springs, New York.

15 Apr.–29 July 1960 MacDowell Colony writers' colony, Peterborough, New Hampshire.

Sept. 1960–June 1961 Apt. 12C, 310 West End Avenue, New York. Stays with Amy Zahl. "Duel in the Kitchen," short story, in *Maclean's* (7 January 1961). Later reprinted as "On Wings of Tongue."

June 1961 Apt. 1, 3765 Dupuis Avenue, Montreal, Quebec. Stays with her sister, Miriam. Boards the *S.S. Demosthenes D,* a coal-carrying freighter, at Brooklyn, New York. Travels through the Panama Canal, along the coast of California, en route to Japan. Wiseman will meet Amy Zahl in Hong Kong; they plan to visit China together. Completes first draft of *The Lovebound* for agent Willis Wing on board ship.

15 June 1961–16 Jan. 1963 Wiseman's literary agent is Willis Kingsley Wing, 24 East 38th Street, New York.

24 July 1961 Arrives in Tokyo, Japan.

27 July 1961 Sends manuscript of *The Lovebound* to Willis Wing.

By 16 Aug–Oct. 1961 In Hong Kong, stays at the Helena May Institute, Garden Road. Awaits news about entry to China, which finally is denied. Meets her travelling companion, Amy Zahl, who arrived prior to Wiseman. During her stay, Zahl has met and become engaged to David Gottlieb, an American scientist. The couple return to London and marry in October. Wiseman is alone for most of her stay in Hong Kong. See "Where Learning Means Hope: Hong Kong's Canadian Club Does What it Can to Aid Worthy Pupils," *Weekend Magazine* (18 May 1963).

21 Aug. 1961 Agent Willis Wing's response to *The Lovebound* is negative.

By 13 Oct. 1961–Apr. 1962 35 Cholmley Gardens, London, England. Stays with Phyllis Gerson, Warden, Stepney Jewish Girls' Club. Visits London to attend Amy Zahl and David Gottlieb's wedding. Becomes seriously ill, requires an operation, and recuperates in London.

16 Apr.–May 1962 Back on Dupuis Avenue, Montreal, with her sister, Miriam.

May 1962–Aug. 1963 490 Burrows Avenue, Winnipeg. Writes stories for children and scripts for broadcast on CBC Radio.

Apr.–July 1963 Essay marker, Department of English, University of Manitoba.

6 Sept. 1963–Apr. 1964 Back on Dupuis Avenue, Montreal, with her sister, Miriam. Part-time teaching position, first-year composition, Department of English, Sir George Williams (now Concordia) University, Montreal. Begins *Crackpot*.

Sept. 1963–Apr. 1969 MacDonald College of McGill University, Montreal. Lecturer, then assistant professor of English.

Nov. 1963 Moves to Apt. 21, 1217 Drummond Street, Montreal.

Feb.–Apr. 1964 Part-time instructor, Institute of Jewish Studies, Snowdon YM-YWHA, Montreal.

Nov. 1964 *Old Markets, New World* (illustrated by Joe Rosenthal) is published by Macmillan of Canada.

1964 Leipzig Book Fair Bronze Medal for *Old Markets, New World*.

Sept. 1966–Apr. 1967 Awarded a Quebec Ministry of Cultural Affairs grant-in-aid ($3000). Takes a one-year unpaid leave from MacDonald College to complete *Crackpot*.

Sept. 1966–Jan. 1967 5975 Southwest 74th Avenue, South Miami, Florida. Stays with her elder brother, Harry.

Feb. 1967 Back on Drummond Street, Montreal.

June 1967 Addresses the Royal Society of Canada, Carleton University, Ottawa, Ontario, at a symposium on "Canada: Past, Present, and Future." Gives a talk, "English Writing in Canada: The Future."

See *Proceedings and Transactions of the Royal Society of Canada*, 4th ser, 5 (June 1967).

July 1967 Has met her future husband, Dmitry Stone, a marine biologist with Beak Consultants Limited. Stone has three sons from a previous marriage.

3 Oct. 1967 Addresses the Faculty of Library and Information Science, University of Toronto, Ontario. Gives a talk on creative writing in Canada.

21–24 Oct. 1967 Festival of the Arts, University of Manitoba. Serves on panel, "In Search of the Modern Novel." Panellists include Jack Ludwig, John Peter, Harold Rosenberg, Wiseman, and Sidney Warhaft as Chair.

Nov. 1967 Wiseman and Stone are living at 2234 Girouard Avenue, Montreal.

12 Mar. 1968–5 Dec. 1969 Wiseman's literary agent is Candida Donadio, first with Russell and Volkening, New York, subsequently with Robert Lantz-Candida Donadio Literary Agency, New York.

4 Apr. 1968 Sends part of the manuscript of *Crackpot* to Candida Donadio.

20 May 1968 Donadio writes an enthusiastic letter in response to *Crackpot* but is unsuccessful in placing the novel with a publisher.

26 June 1969 Tamara Reesa Esther Bliss Stone is born. Wiseman is forty-one.

Aug. 1969 Beak Consultants Limited transfers Stone to Ontario. Wiseman completes her teaching year in April 1969 and resigns from her position at MacDonald College, having chosen to care for Tamara and write. Family moves to 50 Palomino Crescent, Willowdale, Ontario.

Sept. 1969–4 Oct. 1973 Wiseman's literary agent is Matie Molinaro, Canadian Speakers' and Writers' Service, Toronto.

31 Dec. 1969 Wiseman and Stone marry.

17 July 1970 Longman Canada makes an offer to publish *Crackpot*, which later lapses. (Longman contract is signed on 10 October 1970; Wiseman receives a royalty advance of $2000. Molinaro's fee is $200.)

Sept. 1970 Family moves to 29 Monclova Road, Downsview, Ontario.

Oct. 1970 Mounts first *Doll Show*, University of Manitoba.

Oct. 1970–Apr. 1990 Manuscript assessor, Literary Section, Canada Council. Receives $25 per manuscript; then $35; then $45; then $60; then $80.

Summer 1971 Trip to Russia to visit her maternal relatives, in connection with *Old Woman at Play*.

Oct. 1972 Family moves to 1 Rushworth Crescent, Kleinburg, Ontario.

13 Feb. 1973 Mounts *Doll Show*, University of Western Ontario, London.

15–17 June 1973 Attends Conference of Canadian Writers, Toronto (founding of the Writers' Union of Canada).

Sept. 1973–Aug. 1974 Canada Council grant, Explorations Program ($5500). Writes *Testimonial Dinner* and *Old Woman at Play*.

12 Oct. 1973 Jack McClelland of McClelland and Stewart of Toronto invites Wiseman to submit *Crackpot* for consideration.

29 Oct. 1973 McClelland and Stewart offers to publish *Crackpot*. (McClelland and Stewart contract is signed on 15 March 1974;

Wiseman receives a royalty advance of $2000.) McClelland objects strongly to the title but Wiseman will not agree to a change.

Sept. 1974 *Crackpot* is published with a serious misprint on the final page: "previence" for "prurience." The error is corrected immediately. The novel is chosen as an Alternate Selection of the Book of the Month Club, Canada. Promotion tour includes Toronto and Montreal.

1974 Canadian Booksellers Association Award; Montreal Jewish Public Library's J.I. Segal Foundation Award.

1975–76 Writer-in-Residence, Massey College, University of Toronto. Writes *Old Woman at Play*.

21 Jan. 1976 Mounts *Doll Show*, University of Toronto.

11 Feb. 1976 Press Porcépic of Erin, Ontario, makes an offer to publish *The Lovebound* and *Testimonial Dinner*, which it subsequently withdraws.

May 1976 Attends Writers' Union Conference, Ottawa. Family moves to 8 Gosling Road, Maple, Ontario.

Feb. 1977 Wiseman and Stone purchase 324 Rushton Road, Toronto, a former rooming house. Wiseman's elderly parents live with them.

24 Mar. 1977 Mounts *Doll Show*, Centennial Lecture Series, University of Manitoba.

11 Oct. 1977 McClelland and Stewart offers to publish *Old Woman at Play*. Wiseman declines offer.

19–20 Oct. 1977 Participates in "Writers-in-Residence in Conference," University of Toronto.

1978 *Crackpot* is issued by McClelland and Stewart in its New Canadian Library series, number 144, with an introduction by Margaret Laurence.

23 Feb. 1978 Pesach Wiseman dies in Toronto.

May 1978 Clarke, Irwin of Toronto offers to publish *Old Woman at Play*. (Clarke, Irwin contract is dated 21 September 1978; Wiseman receives a royalty advance of $2000.)

1 June 1978 Mounts *Doll Show*, School Librarians' Association, York Memorial Collegiate Institute, Toronto.

Oct. 1978 *Testimonial Dinner* (three-act play) is printed privately for the author by Prototype Press of Toronto.

22 Oct. 1978 Mounts *Doll Show* to promote *Old Woman at Play*, produced by NDWT Company, Bathurst Street Theatre, Toronto. (Wiseman receives a fee of $300.)

25 Nov. 1978 *Old Woman at Play* is published. Promotion tour includes Toronto, London, Ottawa, and Winnipeg.

3–5 May 1979 Conference on Regional Literature, University of Regina, Saskatchewan. Serves on panel, "How Valuable Is Regional Writing?" Panellists include Louis Dudek, Henry Kreisel, Roger Lemelin, and Wiseman.

28 Sept. 1979 "Nursing Explorations: The Experience of Suffering." Centre for Continuing Medical Education, McGill University, Montreal. Gives a talk, "The Spectrum of Suffering."

19–20 Oct. 1979 Participates in workshop, "Language and Literacy in Canada," Toronto.

2 Jan. 1980 Chaika Wiseman dies in Toronto.

Feb. 1980 Participates in Margaret Laurence Program, Saidye Bronfman Centre, Snowdon YM-YWHA, Montreal.

Mar. 1980–Feb. 1983 Canada Council for the Arts Long-Term Grant ($51,000).

12–13 Sept. 1980 Participates in Third Annual *Fireweed* Festival '80, Harbourfront, Toronto.

1981 Jury Chair, English Section (fiction), Governor General's Literary Awards. Jury includes Timothy Findley and W.D. Valgardson.

1981 Excerpts from *The Lovebound: A Tragi-Comedy*; "The Country of the Hungry Bird" (fable), *Journal of Canadian Fiction* 31-32 (1981).

1–14 July 1981 Trip to China with group invited by the Chinese Writers' Association.

See "How to Go to China: (Core Sample from the Continuous Journey)," *Memoirs of a Book Molesting Childhood and Other Essays.*

1982 Jury Member, English Section (fiction), Governor General's Literary Awards. Jury includes Ronald Sutherland and W.D. Valgardson (Chair).

23–24 Apr. 1982 Participates in "Who Do We Think We Are? Canadian Women Writers and Women's Consciousness," Ban Righ Foundation Advisory Council Meeting, Queen's University, Kingston.

24–25 Sept. 1982 1982 Humanities Seminar, "The US and Canadian Border: A Cultural Divide?" South Dakota Committee on the Humanities. Gives a talk, "The Writer and Canadian Literature."

19–29 Oct. 1982 Trip to California sponsored by the Canada Council for the Arts. Gives five readings in the San Francisco Bay area, including Cabrillo College, Kresge College, and Sonoma State College.

1983 Jury Member, English Section (fiction), Governor General's Literary Awards. Jury includes Constance Beresford-Howe (Chair) and W.D. Valgardson.

24–28 Jan. 1983 Writer-in-Residence, Trent University, Peterborough, Ontario.

4–5 Mar. 1983 Participates in Festival of Women's Writing, Open Space Arts Society, Victoria, British Columbia.

1983–84 Writer-in-Residence, Concordia University, Montreal.

23 Oct. 1983 Launch of *Old Woman at Play* (videocassette), 28 min., produced by Howard Rypp, Nephesh Theatre, Harbourfront, Toronto.

5 Dec. 1983 Porcupine's Quill of Erin, Ontario, makes an offer to publish *Memoirs of a Book Molesting Childhood and Other Essays*, which it subsequently withdraws.

1984–85 Three Guineas Charitable Foundation Agency Award ($20,000). Writes poetry (never published).

1985, 1986 Edits *The Canadian Women Writers Engagement Calendar* (Toronto: Yewdewit Books).

14–20 July 1985 Participates in Maritime Writers' Workshop, University of New Brunswick, Fredericton.

23 Sept. 1985 Porcupine's Quill offers to publish *Kenji and the Cricket* (originally titled *Miko and the Crickets*). (Porcupine's Quill contract is dated 7 June 1988; Wiseman receives a royalty advance of $1050.)

Dec. 1985 Creative Artists in Schools Project, Ontario Arts Council grant ($1593).

Mar. 1986 Ontario Arts Council grant ($500).

6 June 1986 Oxford University Press of Toronto offers to publish *Memoirs of a Book Molesting Childhood and Other Essays*. (Oxford University Press contract is dated 24 June 1986; Wiseman receives a royalty advance of $3000.)

4–6 July 1986 Participates in "Out of the Everywhere/Voyage au coeur du récit," Canadian Pavilion, Expo '86, Vancouver, British Columbia.

1986–87 Writer-in-Residence, University of Western Ontario, London.

27–29 Oct. 1986 Conference on "L'homme et la forêt," Université de Dijon, France. Gives a talk, "And the Forest?" See *Memoirs of a Book Molesting Childhood and Other Essays*.

4 Jan. 1987 Margaret Laurence dies in Lakefield, Ontario.

31 Mar.–8 Apr. 1987 Participates in "International Conference of Women Writers," Jerusalem, Israel.

Summer 1987–91 Head, May Writing Studios, Banff Centre for the Arts, Alberta. The Banff Centre has since established the Adele Wiseman Scholarship.

Fall 1987 Writer-in-Residence, University of Prince Edward Island, Charlottetown.

Oct. 1987 *Memoirs of a Book Molesting Childhood and Other Essays* (Studies in Canadian Literature series) is published by Oxford University Press.

1988 Montreal Jewish Public Library's J.I. Segal Foundation Award. *Kenji and the Cricket* (children's book), illustrated by Shiuye Takashima, is published by Porcupine's Quill. Wiseman writes the afterword to Margaret Laurence's *The Stone Angel*, issued by McClelland and Stewart in its New Canadian Library series. (Wiseman receives a fee of $400.)

22–24 Jan. 1988 Panellist, Canadian Women Writers Seminar, "Stars out of the North/Les étoiles du nord," College of St. Catherine, St. Paul, Minnesota.

10–12 Mar. 1988 Wiseman opens the Margaret Laurence Tribute, Trent University, with the first annual Margaret Laurence Lecture.

21 Mar. 1988 Participates in "The Adaskin Years: A Conference on Canada's Arts, 1930–1970," University of Victoria, British Columbia.

28–30 July 1988 Participates in "Women and the Arts/Les femmes et les arts," Spotlight '88, Winnipeg.

1988–91 Writer-in-Residence, University of Windsor, Ontario. The University of Windsor has since established the Adele Wiseman Poetry Award. Open to students in creative writing workshops, the award is valued at $100 and the winning poem is published in the *University of Windsor Review*.

19 Oct. 1989 LLD (honorary), University of Manitoba.

1990 Wiseman and Stone divorce.

21–25 Nov. 1991 Visits Acadia University, Wolfville, Nova Scotia. Reads from *Memoirs of a Book Molesting Childhood and Other Essays.*

Mar. 1992 "Goon of the Moon and the Expendables" (short story), *Malahat Review* 98 (March 1992).

1 June 1992 Adele Wiseman dies in Toronto from complications related to sarcoma.

24 June 1992 Memorial tribute to Wiseman, Factory Theatre, Toronto.

1992 *Puccini and the Prowlers* (children's book), illustrated by Kim Lafave, is published by Nightwood Editions of Toronto.

1993 *Malahat Review* receives Western Magazine Award for Fiction for Wiseman's short story, "Goon of the Moon and the Expendables."

2–26 Feb. 1995 *Crackpot*, play by Rachel Wyatt, directed by Martin Fishman. Alberta Theatre Projects, playRites '95 Festival, Calgary. Based on Wiseman's novel.

26 Oct. 2003 *On Wings of Tongue*, play by Ann Powell and Suzanne Hersh. Buddies in Bad Times Theatre, Toronto. Based on Wiseman's short story.

24 Oct. 2004 *On Wings of Tongue*, play by Ann Powell and Suzanne Hersh. Miles Nadal Jewish Community Centre, Toronto. Based on Wiseman's short story.

Adele Wiseman:
Principal Publications

1956 *The Sacrifice*. New York: Viking Press; Toronto: Macmillan; London: Victor Gollancz. [novel]

c1960 *The Lovebound: A Tragi-Comedy*. Printed privately for the author. [two-act play]

1964 *Old Markets, New World*. Illus. Joe Rosenthal. Toronto: Macmillan. [non-fiction]

1974 *Crackpot*. Toronto: McClelland and Stewart. [novel]

1978 *Old Woman at Play*. Toronto: Clarke, Irwin. [non-fiction]

1978 *Testimonial Dinner*. Toronto: Prototype Press. Printed privately for the author. [three-act play]

1987 *Memoirs of a Book Molesting Childhood and Other Essays*. Studies in Canadian Literature. Toronto: Oxford University Press. [essays]

1988 *Kenji and the Cricket*. Illus. Shizuye Takashima. Erin: Porcupine's Quill. [children's book]

1992 *Puccini and the Prowlers*. Illus. Kim Lafave. Toronto: Nightwood Editions. [children's book]

1997 *Selected Letters of Margaret Laurence and Adele Wiseman*. Ed. John Lennox and Ruth Panofsky. Toronto: University of Toronto Press. [correspondence]

PREFACE

[1] James L.W. West, III, *American Authors and the Literary Marketplace since 1900* (Philadelphia: University of Pennsylvania Press, 1988), 5.

[2] Frank Davey, "Writers and Publishers in English–Canadian Literature," in *Reading Canadian Reading* (Winnipeg: Turnstone Press, 1988), 94.

[3] See, for example, Elspeth Cameron, *Earle Birney: A Life* (Toronto: Viking Press, 1994); Joan Givner, *Mazo de la Roche: The Hidden Life* (Toronto: Oxford University Press, 1989); Judith Skelton Grant, *Robertson Davies: Man of Myth* (Toronto: Viking Press, 1994); James King, *The Life of Margaret Laurence* (Toronto: Alfred A. Knopf Canada, 1997); James King, *Farley: The Life of Farley Mowat* (Toronto HarperFlamingoCanada, 2002); Ira B. Nadel, *Various Positions: A Life of Leonard Cohen* (Toronto: Random House, 1996); François Ricard, *Gabrielle Roy, une vie: biographie* (Montréal: Boréal, 1996); Rosemary Sullivan, *By Heart: Elizabeth Smart, A Life* (Toronto: Penguin Books Canada, 1991); Rosemary Sullivan, *Shadow Maker: The Life of Gwendolyn MacEwen* (Toronto: HarperCollins, 1996); Rosemary Sullivan, *The Red Shoes: Margaret Atwood Starting Out* (Toronto: HarperCollins, 1998); and Patrick Toner, *If I Could Turn and*

Meet Myself: The Life of Alden Nowlan (Fredericton: Goose Lane Editions, 2000). Biographers David Stouck and Robert Thacker, however, draw extensively on archival material to probe the publishing careers of Ethel Wilson, Sinclair Ross, and Alice Munro. See David Stouck, *Ethel Wilson: A Critical Biography* (Toronto: University of Toronto Press, 2003); David Stouck, *As for Sinclair Ross* (Toronto: University of Toronto Press, 2005); and Robert Thacker, *Alice Munro, Writing Her Lives: A Biography* (Toronto: McClelland and Stewart, 2005).

[4] Francess Halpenny, "From Author to Reader," in *Literary History of Canada*, gen. ed. W.H. New, third edition, volume 4 (Toronto: University of Toronto Press, 1990), 404.

[5] Ibid.

[6] Travis DeCook, "The History of the Book, Literary History, and Identity Politics in Canada," *Studies in Canadian Literature* 27, 2 (2002): 81.

[7] Carole Gerson, "The Canadian Publishers' Records Database and Canadian Book History," address, Bibliographical Society of Canada, 28 June 2004, p. 6.

[8] Ibid., 7.

[9] Qtd. in ibid., 5–6.

[10] See Patricia Lockhart Fleming and Yvan Lamonde, gen. eds., *History of the Book in Canada*, 3 volumes (Toronto: University of Toronto Press, 2004–2007); Roy MacSkimming, *The Perilous Trade: Publishing Canada's Writers* (Toronto: McClelland and Stewart, 2003); Bruce Whiteman, *Lasting Impressions: A Short History of English Publishing in Quebec* (Montréal: Véhicule Press, 1994); Roy MacSkimming, *Making Literary History: House of Anansi Press 1967–1997* (Concord: House of Anansi Press, 1997); Paul Grescoe, *The Merchants of Venus: Inside Harlequin and the Empire of Romance* (Vancouver: Raincoast Books, 1996); James King, *Jack, A Life with Writers: The Story of Jack McClelland* (Toronto: Alfred A. Knopf Canada, 1999); Sam Solecki, ed., *Imagining Canadian Literature: The Selected Letters of Jack McClelland* (Toronto: Key Porter Books, 1998); Nick Mount, *When Canadian Literature Moved to New York* (Toronto: University of Toronto Press, 2005); Clarence Karr, *Authors and Audiences: Popular Canadian Fiction in the Early Twentieth Century*

(Montreal: McGill-Queen's University Press, 2000); JoAnn McCaig, *Reading in Alice Munro's Archives* (Waterloo: Wilfrid Laurier University Press, 2002); and *Studies in Canadian Literature* 25, 1 (2000).

[11] Francess Halpenny, "Bibliography: The Foundation of Scholarship," in *Symposium on Scholarly Communication: Papers Delivered at the Symposium Held in Ottawa in October 1980* (Ottawa: Aid to Scholarly Publications Programme, 1981), 42.

[12] I discuss this matter further in the following article: Ruth Panofsky and Michael Moir, "Halted by the Archive: The Impact of Excessive Archival Restrictions on Scholars," *Journal of Scholarly Publishing* 37, 1 (October 2005): 19–32.

INTRODUCTION

[1] Adele Wiseman, *Memoirs of a Book Molesting Childhood and Other Essays*, Studies in Canadian Literature (Toronto: Oxford University Press, 1987), 51, 52. Subsequent quotations from this book are cited in the chapter as page references in brackets in the text.

CHAPTER 1

[1] See Marcia Mack, "*The Sacrifice* and *Crackpot*: What a Woman Can Learn by Rewriting a Fairy Tale and Clarifying Its Meaning," *Essays on Canadian Writing* 68 (Spring 1999): 134–58; and Ruth Panofsky, "From Complicity to Subversion: The Female Subject in Adele Wiseman's Novels," *Canadian Literature* 137 (Spring 1993): 41–48, rpt. in Panofsky, ed., *Adele Wiseman: Essays on Her Works*, Writers Series 7 (Toronto: Guernica Editions, 2001), 55–67.

[2] Wiseman, *Memoirs*, 61.

[3] Adele Wiseman, "A Brief Anatomy of an Honest Attempt at a Pithy Statement about the Impact of the Manitoba Environment on My Development as an Artist," *Mosaic* 3, 3 (Spring 1970): 105.

[4] Wiseman, *Memoirs*, 49.

[5] Ibid., 7.

[6] Adele Wiseman, *Old Woman at Play* (Toronto: Clarke, Irwin, 1978), 145.

[7] Miriam Dorn, personal interview, 21 April 2001.

[8] Wiseman, *Old Woman*, 28–29.

[9] Wiseman, *Memoirs*, 29.

[10] Ibid., 29.

[11] Wiseman, *Old Woman*, 145.

[12] Ibid.

[13] Tamara Stone, "A Memoir of My Mother," in *We Who Can Fly: Poems, Essays and Memories in Honour of Adele Wiseman*, ed. Elizabeth Greene (Dunvegan: Cormorant Books, 1997), 43.

[14] Sidney Perlmutter, personal interview, 1 December 1999.

[15] Wiseman, *Memoirs*, 8.

[16] Perlmutter, personal interview.

[17] Wiseman, *Memoirs*, 25.

[18] Ibid., 26.

[19] Throughout the 1920s until the early 1960s, special admission requirements and restrictive quotas for Jewish students were in place across Canadian universities. Wiseman's eldest sibling, Miriam, for example, was refused admission to the Faculty of Medicine at the University of Manitoba. She went on to pursue doctoral studies in chemistry at McGill University and became a professor of chemistry at McGill.

[20] John Speers, personal interview, 11 November 1999.

[21] Beverley Slopen, "Malcolm Ross: Caretaker of CanLit," *Quill and Quire* (May 1978): 22.

[22] David Staines, Introduction, *The Impossible Sum of Our Traditions: Reflections on Canadian Literature*, by Malcolm Ross (Toronto: McClelland and Stewart, 1986), 15.

[23] Slopen, "Malcolm Ross," 21.

[24] Malcolm Ross, telephone interview, 14 October 1999.

[25] Staines, Introduction, 11.

[26] Diana Hume George, "A Vision of My Obscured Soul," *Ohio Review* 51 (1994): 46.

[27] Malcolm Ross to Wiseman, 5 November 1991, Wiseman fonds.

[28] George, "A Vision," 52.

[29] Kathryn Chittick, "*SCL* Interviews: Malcolm Ross," *Studies in Canadian Literature* 9, 2 (Summer 1984): 255.

[30] Staines, Introduction, 11.

[31] Ross, telephone interview.

[32] Ibid.

[33] Bruce Meyer and Brian O'Riordan, "The Permissible and the Possible: Adele Wiseman," in *Lives and Works: Interviews* (Windsor: Black Moss Press, 1992), 124.

[34] Ibid., 125.

[35] Wiseman, *Memoirs*, 51.

[36] Ibid., 50.

[37] David Lazar, "On Mentorship," *Ohio Review* 51 (1994): 32.

[38] Deborah Digges, "The Waiting Room Door," *Ohio Review* 51 (1994): 113.

[39] Wiseman fonds.

[40] John Lennox and Ruth Panofsky, eds., *Selected Letters of Margaret Laurence and Adele Wiseman* (Toronto: University of Toronto Press, 1997), 197.

[41] Carole Gerson, "The Canon between the Wars: Field-Notes of a Feminist Literary Archaeologist," in *Canadian Canons: Essays in Literary Value*, ed. Robert Lecker (Toronto: University of Toronto Press, 1991), 47.

[42] Gail Scott, *Spaces like stairs* (Toronto: Women's Press, 1989), 67.

[43] Wiseman speculated that Laurence likely discarded her friend's letters while still in West Africa. Adele Wiseman suggested this possibility to the author.

[44] Lennox and Panofsky, eds., *Selected Letters*, 33.

[45] Ibid., 40.

[46] Margaret Laurence to Wiseman, 19 July 1950, in Lennox and Panofsky, eds., *Selected Letters*, 41.

[47] Laurence to Wiseman, ibid., 42.

[48] Wiseman to Laurence, ibid., 290.

[49] Adrienne Rich, *On Lies, Secrets, and Silences: Selected Prose 1966–1978* (New York: Norton, 1979), 38.

[50] Ibid., 208.

[51] Carol Shields, "Brave Bulletins from the Mother Zone," rev. of *The Mother Zone: Love, Sex and Laundry in the Modern Family*, by Marni Jackson, *Globe and Mail*, 17 October 1992, p. C24.

[52] Wiseman to Laurence, in Lennox and Panofsky, eds., *Selected Letters*, 281–82.

[53] Laurence to Wiseman, 17 April 1969, in ibid., 292.

[54] Laurence to Wiseman, ibid., 114.

[55] Laurence to Wiseman, ibid., 156–57.

[56] Laurence to Wiseman, 8 October 1961, in ibid., 138.

[57] Laurence to Wiseman, ibid., 261.

[58] Laurence to Wiseman, 3 September 1968, in ibid., 261–62.

[59] Wiseman to Laurence, 23 September 1968, in ibid., 268–69.

[60] Rich, *On Lies*, 214.

[61] Wiseman enjoyed enduring friendships with Marian Engel, Sylvia Fraser, Phyllis Grosskurth, Basya Hunter, Joy Kogawa, Betty Lambert, Joyce Marshall, Anne Michaels, Janis Rapoport, Chava Rosenfarb, Colleen Thibaudeau, Miriam Waddington, Helen Weinzweig, and Rachel Wyatt in Canada; Joanne Greenberg (aka Hannah Green) and Tillie Olsen in the United States; and Ding Ling in China. Wiseman felt slight kinship with contemporary male writers such as Mordecai Richler and Philip Roth, for example, whose Jewish sensibilities differed markedly from her own.

[62] Malcolm Ross to Wiseman, 6 January 1987, Wiseman fonds.

[63] Wiseman, *Memoirs*, 184.

[64] Adele Wiseman, "Writing in Ontario: Up and Doing," *Hungry Mind Review: A Midwestern Book Review* 10 (Spring 1989): 8.

[65] Margaret Laurence, *Dance on the Earth: A Memoir* (Toronto: McClelland and Stewart, 1989), 76.

[66] Mordecai Richler, personal interview, 19 November 1999.

[67] She definitely attended the occasional concert and play, including a performance of T.S. Eliot's *The Cocktail Party*. The following year in Rome, moreover, Wiseman came to know some members of the expatriate North American community, including the rising Jewish-American literary and cultural critic Leslie Fiedler and his wife, for whom she babysat.

Wiseman herself admitted that during Margaret Laurence's "years in Africa we corresponded constantly, mainly about our work, which we knew (though the world as yet remained regrettably ignorant) was writing" (*Memoirs*, 51). Laurence lived in Africa for a total of six years between late 1950 and early 1957, a period that coincided with the composition and publication of *The Sacrifice*, a time of intense activity for Wiseman. No doubt, given the open and personal nature of their extant correspondence, Wiseman's earliest letters to her friend would have contained valuable details about her time in London. See Lennox and Panofsky, eds., *Selected Letters*. For the complete correspondence, see the Adele Wiseman fonds and the Margaret Laurence fonds, Clara Thomas Archives, Scott Library, York University.

[68] Laurence to Wiseman, 27 December 1950, in Lennox and Panofsky, eds., *Selected Letters*, 47.

[69] Laurence to Wiseman, 12 February 1951, in ibid., 51.

[70] Laurence to Wiseman, 2 May 1951, in ibid., 51.

[71] Laurence to Wiseman, 15 June 1951, in ibid., 54.

[72] Laurence to Wiseman, 9 November 1951, in ibid., 66.

[73] Laurence to Wiseman, ibid., 70.

[74] Laurence to Wiseman, 30 January 1952, in ibid., 70.

[75] Laurence to Wiseman, ibid., 74.

[76] Laurence to Wiseman, 1 December 1952, in ibid., 78.

[77] Wiseman, *Memoirs*, 59, 60.

[78] Ibid., 52.

[79] Laurence to Wiseman, 16 February 1953, in Lennox and Panofsky, eds., *Selected Letters*, 79.

[80] Laurence to Wiseman, 8 June 1953, in ibid., 83.

[81] Laurence to Wiseman, 14 December 1953, in ibid., 85.

[82] Laurence to Wiseman, 7 April 1954, in ibid., 88.

[83] Robert Weaver, personal interview, 6 April 2000.

[84] Sandy Stewart, *From Coast to Coast: A Personal History of Radio in Canada* (Toronto: CBC, 1985), 155.

[85] George Woodcock, "Weaver, Robert," in *The Oxford Companion to Canadian Literature*, ed. Eugene Benson and William Toye, second edition (Toronto: Oxford University Press, 1997), 1172.

[86] McCaig, *Reading in Alice Munro's Archives*, 27.

[87] Robert Weaver to Wiseman, 26 October 1949, Weaver fonds.

[88] Weaver to Wiseman, 19 July 1950, ibid.

[89] Weaver to Wiseman, 9 May 1950, ibid.

[90] Weaver edited the literary quarterly *Tamarack Review* along with Kildare Dobbs, Millar MacLure, Ivon Owen, William Toye, and Anne Wilkinson.

[91] Weaver to Wiseman, 21 July 1959, Weaver fonds.

[92] Weaver, personal interview.

[93] Ibid.

[94] Weaver to Wiseman, 31 January 1958, Weaver fonds.

[95] Laurence to Wiseman, 25 June 1964, in Lennox and Panofsky, eds., *Selected Letters*, 174.

[96] Weaver, personal interview.

[97] Laurence to Wiseman, 10 July 1956, in Lennox and Panofsky, eds., *Selected Letters*, 92.

[98] Ross to Wiseman, 23 February 1961, Wiseman fonds.

[99] Ross to Wiseman, 30 August [1955], ibid.

[100] Ross to Wiseman, 13 July [1954], ibid.

101 Wiseman to Laurence, 29 June 1955, in Lennox and Panofsky, eds., *Selected Letters*, 89.

102 Laurence to Wiseman, 20 June 1955, in ibid., 89.

103 Weaver, personal interview.

104 Ibid.

105 The conference was held 28 to 31 July 1955. The writers in attendance included Earle Birney, Morley Callaghan, Leonard Cohen, Louis Dudek, Ralph Gustafson, Irving Layton, Dorothy Livesay, Jay Macpherson, Eli Mandel, James Reaney, Al Purdy, F.R. Scott, A.J.M. Smith, John Sutherland, Miriam Waddington, and Phyllis Webb.

106 Jack McClelland to Wiseman, 9 July 1954, Wiseman fonds.

107 Ross, telephone interview.

108 Weaver, personal interview.

109 Ross, telephone interview.

110 Kildare Dobbs to Willis Kingsley Wing, 24 April 1962, Curtis Brown Ltd. archives; Kildare Dobbs, personal interview, 8 November 1999.

111 Marshall Ayres Best to John Morgan Gray, 17 November 1955, Macmillan fonds.

112 Best to Gray, 2 September 1955, ibid.

113 Dobbs, personal interview.

114 Dobbs to Wiseman, 17 October 1955, Macmillan fonds.

115 Howard Engel, "Dobbs, Kildare," in *The Oxford Companion to Canadian Literature*, ed. Eugene Benson and William Toye, second edition (Toronto: Oxford University Press, 1997), 297.

116 Dobbs to Wiseman, 4 October 1955, Macmillan fonds.

117 Dobbs to Wiseman, 20 July 1956, ibid.

118 Dobbs to Wiseman, 5 October 1956, ibid.

119 John Morgan Gray, "Canadian Books: A Publisher's View," *Canadian Literature* 33 (Summer 1967): 35.

120 Dobbs to Wiseman, 17 October 1955, Macmillan fonds.

121 Ibid.

[122] Ibid.

[123] Dobbs to Wiseman, 20 August 1956, ibid.

[124] Dobbs to Wiseman, 18 September 1956, ibid.

[125] Dobbs to Wiseman, 2 May 1957, ibid.

[126] Dobbs to Wiseman, 14 May 1957, ibid.

[127] Dobbs, personal interview.

[128] Dobbs to Wiseman, 4 December 1956, Macmillan fonds.

[129] Ibid.

[130] Dobbs to Wiseman, 18 September 1956, ibid.

[131] Dobbs to Wiseman, 2 May 1957, ibid.

[132] Ibid.

[133] Dobbs, personal interview.

[134] Ibid.

[135] John Morgan Gray, *Fun Tomorrow: Learning to Be a Publisher and Much Else* (Toronto: Macmillan, 1978), 240.

[136] Lovat Dickson, "Gray, John Morgan," in *The Oxford Companion to Canadian Literature*, ed. Eugene Benson and William Toye, second edition (Toronto: Oxford University Press, 1997), 492–93.

[137] Delores Brotten and Peter Birdsall, *Paper Phoenix: A History of Book Publishing in English Canada* (Victoria: Canlit, 1980), 23.

[138] W.H. New, *A History of Canadian Literature* (Montreal: McGill-Queen's University Press, 1989), 181.

[139] *The Reminiscences of Marshall Ayres Best* (1976), Oral History Research Collection, Rare Book and Manuscript Library, Columbia University, 153.

[140] Gray to Best, 8 September 1955, Macmillan fonds.

[141] Gray to Best, 7 October 1955, ibid.

[142] M.A.B., 15 February 1956, ibid.

[143] Best to Wiseman, Wiseman fonds.

[144] Best and Wiseman to Gray, 4 August 1956, Macmillan fonds.

[145] Gray to Juliet Piggott, 21 November 1955, Macmillan fonds.

[146] Victor Gollancz to Wiseman, 22 March 1956, Wiseman fonds.

[147] Wiseman fonds.

[148] Jean Richardson, "Gollancz: The House that Victor Built," *British Book News* (June 1989): 396.

[149] See Ruth Dudley Edwards, *Victor Gollancz: A Biography* (London: Victor Gollancz, 1987).

[150] Best to Wiseman, 19 October 1956, Wiseman fonds.

[151] Weaver, personal interview.

[152] M.M. Mitchell, "Saturday Review of Books: Ukrainian Jews Try New Life in Winnipeg," *Globe and Mail* [Toronto], 6 October 1956, p. 5.

[153] James Scott, "The Abraham Story: New Author Rises on Canadian Scene," *Telegram* [Toronto], 15 September 1956, p. 34.

[154] Lawrence Sabbath, "New Outlook to an Old Tradition," *Gazette* [Montreal], 29 September 1956, p. 31.

[155] J[oe] M. G[elman], "A Saturday Review: New Books and Old. Greatness Achieved," *Winnipeg Free Press*, 29 September 1956, p. 9.

[156] Mack, "What a Woman Can Learn," 135.

[157] Orville Prescott, "Books of the Times," *New York Times*, 14 September 1956, p. 21.

[158] Winfield Townley Scott, "Modern Scene, Biblical Echoes in a Fine, Mature First Novel," *New York Herald Tribune*, 16 September 1956, p. 1.

[159] Saul Maloff, "Books and Comment: The World of Double Exile," *New Republic*, 12 November 1956, p. 21.

[160] "New Fiction," rev. of *Destination Berlin*, by Paul Vialar, trans. Philip John Stead; *The Sacrifice*, by Adele Wiseman; *Splendid Sunday*, by James Ambrose Brown; *The Last Resort*, by Pamela Hansford Johnson; and *Ferguson*, by Rayne Kruger, *Times* [London], 8 November 1956, p. 13.

[161] "Thorny Paths," rev. of *The Sacrifice*, by Adele Wiseman; *Peter Perry*, by Michael Campbell; and *The Angel in the Corner*, by Monica Dickens, *Times Literary Supplement*, 9 November 1956, p. 661.

[162] Christina Kurata, personal interview, 21 June 2001.

[163] Scott, "Abraham Story," 34.

[164] Mack, "What a Woman Can Learn," 138.

[165] Adele Wiseman, *The Sacrifice* (Toronto: Macmillan, 1956), 344.

[166] Wiseman, *Memoirs*, 58–59.

[167] 2 September 1955, Macmillan fonds.

CHAPTER TWO

[1] Qtd. in Meyer and O'Riordan, "Permissable," 127.

[2] Gabriella Morisco, "The Charm of an Unorthodox Feminism: An Interview with Adele Wiseman," in *We Who Can Fly: Poems, Essays and Memories in Honour of Adele Wiseman*, ed. Elizabeth Greene (Dunvegan: Cormorant Books, 1997), 141.

[3] Mack, "What a Woman Can Learn," 156.

[4] Roslyn Belkin, "The Consciousness of a Jewish Artist: An Interview with Adele Wiseman," *Journal of Canadian Fiction* 31–32 (1981): 161.

[5] Ibid.

[6] Meyer and O'Riordan, "Permissible," 124.

[7] Belkin, "Consciousness," 161.

[8] Wiseman to Laurence, 8 May 1968, in Lennox and Panofsky, eds., *Selected Letters*, p. 246.

[9] Belkin, "Consciousness," 161.

[10] Ibid.

[11] Meyer, "Permissible," 124.

[12] Belkin, "Consciousness," 62.

[13] See *Kenji and the Cricket*, illus. Shizuye Takashima (Erin: Porcupine's Quill, 1988); and *Puccini and the Prowlers*, illus. Kim Lafave (Toronto: Nightwood Editions, 1992).

[14] On 29 May 1963, "My Burglar" was broadcast on CBC Winnipeg's *Prairie Talks*. In late June 1963, Wiseman recorded five talks for CBC Winnipeg about an aborted trip to China, two of

which were "Junk Hunting at Home and Abroad" and "On Food and Eating." She was paid fifty-five dollars for each recording.

[15] Laurence to Wiseman, in Lennox and Panofsky, eds., *Selected Letters*, 189.

[16] Adele Freedman, "The Stubborn Ethnicity of Adele W.," *Saturday Night* (May 1976): 27.

[17] Laurence to Wiseman, 24 January 1965, in Lennox and Panofsky, eds., *Selected Letters*, 194.

[18] Eleanor Wachtel, "Profile: Voice of the Prophet," *Books in Canada* (October 1984): 12-13.

[19] Laurence to Wiseman, in Lennox and Panofsky, eds., *Selected Letters*, 201.

[20] Wachtel, "Profile," 12.

[21] Wiseman to Laurence, 27 October 1965, in Lennox and Panofsky, eds., *Selected Letters*, 205–06.

[22] Chava Rosenfarb, personal interview, 25 October 2000.

[23] Laurence to Wiseman, 24 January 1966, in Lennox and Panofsky, eds., *Selected Letters*, 209.

[24] Wiseman to Laurence, 7 July 1966, in ibid., 210.

[25] Ibid., 217.

[26] Wiseman to Laurence, 17 July 1967, in ibid., 222.

[27] Wiseman to Laurence, 27 August 1967, in ibid., 224–25.

[28] Ibid., 236–37.

[29] Wiseman to Laurence, 2 February 1968, in ibid., 237.

[30] Wiseman to Laurence, 31 March 1968, in ibid., 239.

[31] Belkin, "Consciousness," 161.

[32] *The Lovebound: A Tragi-Comedy* was printed privately for the author in 1960. Copyright was registered in Canada on 2 April 1964, and in the United States on 1 February 1965. Excerpts appeared in the *Journal of Canadian Fiction* 31–32 (1981): 140–47.

In 1973, *The Lovebound* was rejected by House of Anansi Press in Toronto. In 1976, Press Porcépic of Erin, Ontario, made an offer to publish *The Lovebound* and *Testimonial Dinner* (Wiseman's second play), which it subsequently withdrew. *Testimonial Dinner* was printed privately for the author in 1978. *The Lovebound* and *Testimonial Dinner* are accessible in the Adele Wiseman fonds, Clara Thomas Archives, Scott Library, York University.

[33] Wiseman's interest in China began in childhood. See Wiseman, "Where Learning Means Hope: Hong Kong's Canadian Club Does What it Can to Aid Worthy Pupils," *Weekend Magazine* (18 May 1963): 18+; and Wiseman, "How to Go to China," in *Chinada: Memoirs of the Gang of Seven*, by Gary Geddes, Geoff Hancock, Robert Kroetsch, Patrick Lane, Alice Munro, Suzanne Paradis, and Adele Wiseman (Dunvegan: Quadrant Press, 1982), 98–128.

[34] Wiseman to Laurence, 8 May 1968, in Lennox and Panofsky, eds., *Selected Letters*, 245.

[35] Laurence to Wiseman, 13 May 1968, in ibid., 247.

[36] Wiseman to Laurence, 8 May 1968, in ibid., 245.

[37] Laurence to Wiseman, 30 June 1968, in ibid., 258.

[38] Wiseman to Laurence, 8 May 1968, in ibid., 245.

[39] Ibid.

[40] Wiseman to Laurence, 29 May 1968, in ibid., 250.

[41] Gray, *Fun,* 139.

[42] Bruce Whiteman, Charlotte Stewart, and Catherine Funnell, *A Bibliography of Macmillan of Canada Imprints 1906–1980* (Toronto: Dundurn Press, 1985), xii–xiii.

[43] Dickson, "Gray," 492.

[44] Gray was co-editor (with Frank A. Upjohn) of *Prose of Our Day* (Toronto: Macmillan, 1940); and author of *A.W. Mackenzie, The Grove, Lakefield: A Memoir* (Toronto: Grove Old Boys' Association, 1938); *The One-Eyed Trapper* (Toronto: Macmillan, 1942), a book for children; *Lord Selkirk of Red River* (Toronto: Macmillan, 1963), awarded the University of British Columbia medal for best biography of the year; *Fun Tomorrow: Learning to Be a Publisher and Much Else* (Toronto: Macmillan, 1978), a memoir; and numerous articles on publishing.

[45] Dickson, "Gray," 492.

[46] Bruce Whiteman, "The Archive of the Macmillan Company of Canada Ltd. Part I: 1905–1965," *Library Research News* [McMaster University Library] 8, 1 (Spring 1984): vii.

[47] Gray to Wiseman, 22 February 1956, Macmillan fonds.

[48] Gray to Wiseman, 1 March 1956, ibid.

[49] Gray to Wiseman, 2 May 1957, ibid.

[50] Gray to Wiseman, 7 November 1956, ibid.

[51] Gray to Henry Allen Moe, 17 December 1956, ibid.

[52] Dobbs, personal interview.

[53] Ibid.

[54] Gray to Wiseman, 6 September 1960, Macmillan fonds.

[55] Gray to Wiseman, 30 November 1960, ibid.

[56] Gray to Wiseman, 15 December 1960, ibid.

[57] Gray to Wiseman, 1 February 1961, ibid.

[58] Freedman, "Stubborn," 27.

[59] Ross to Wiseman, 23 February 1961, Wiseman fonds.

[60] Freedman, "Stubborn," 27.

[61] Ibid.

[62] Ibid.

[63] Ibid.

[64] Gray to Best, 19 October 1963, Macmillan fonds.

[65] Best to Gray, 26 October 1962, ibid.

[66] *Telegram* [Toronto], 28 January 1961, p. 46. The advertisement was refused by the *Vancouver Sun* and the *Winnipeg Tribune*.

[67] Wing to Wiseman, 19 April 1962, Curtis Brown Ltd. archives.

[68] Gray to Best, 19 October 1962, Macmillan fonds.

[69] Gray to Wiseman, 31 May 1961, ibid.

[70] Gray to Wiseman, 13 October 1961, ibid.

[71] Qtd. in Laurence to Wiseman, 5 September 1961, in Lennox and Panofsky, eds., *Selected Letters*, 136.

[72] Best to Gray, 26 October 1962, Macmillan fonds.

[73] Gray to Wing, 12 November 1962, Macmillan fonds.

[74] Wiseman, *The Lovebound*, 67–68.

[75] Gray to Wing, 12 November 1962, Macmillan fonds.

[76] Gray to Wiseman, 15 November 1962, ibid.

[77] Gray to Wiseman, 21 August 1963, ibid.

[78] Robert Fulford, "But Why Own It?" rev. of *Canada*, photog. Peter Varley, introd. Kildare Dobbs; and *Old Markets, New World*, text Adele Wiseman, illus. Joe Rosenthal, *Toronto Daily Star*, 21 November 1964, p. 26.

[79] 9 March 1963, Macmillan fonds.

[80] Qtd. in Wiseman to Laurence, 14 August 1968, in Lennox and Panofsky, eds., *Selected Letters*, 259.

[81] Ibid.

[82] Dobbs, personal interview.

[83] Wiseman to Laurence, 14 August 1968, in Lennox and Panofsky, eds., *Selected Letters*, 259.

[84] Ibid.

[85] Qtd. in Wiseman to Laurence, 4–5 September 1968, in ibid., 265.

[86] Wiseman to Laurence, 4–5 September 1968, in ibid., 265.

[87] Wiseman to Laurence, 23 September 1968, in ibid., 269.

[88] Wiseman to Laurence, 12 October 1968, in ibid., 273.

[89] Wiseman to Laurence, 23 September 1968, in ibid., 269.

[90] In the United States, *Crackpot* was rejected by Atlantic Monthly; Crown; Doubleday; Farrar, Straus and Giroux; Grove; Harcourt, Brace and World; Harper and Row; Holt, Rinehart and Winston; Houghton Mifflin; Alfred A. Knopf; Meredith; William Morrow; Praeger; Random House; Charles Scribner's Sons; Simon and Schuster; and Viking. In Great Britain, the novel was rejected by

W.H. Allen; Andre Deutsch; Victor Gollancz; George G. Harrap; and Michael Joseph; and in Canada by House of Anansi; Longman; and Macmillan.

[91] Ross to Wiseman, Thursday [1969], Wiseman fonds.

[92] 24 April 1969, Macmillan fonds.

[93] L.S., undated report, Macmillan fonds.

[94] Gray to Wiseman, 27 May 1969, ibid.

[95] Wiseman to Laurence, 12 June 1969, in Lennox and Panofsky, eds., *Selected Letters*, 304–05.

[96] Wiseman to Gray, 17 July 1969, Macmillan fonds.

[97] Gray to Wiseman, 25 July 1969, ibid.

[98] Wiseman to Laurence, 28 July 1969, in Lennox and Panofsky, eds., *Selected Letters*, 308.

[99] Gray to Wiseman, Macmillan fonds.

[100] Wiseman to Laurence, 28 July 1969, in Lennox and Panofsky, eds., *Selected Letters*, 308.

[101] See "From *Crackpot*," in *Canadian Writing Today*, ed. Mordecai Richler (Harmondsworth: Penguin, 1970), 233–45.

[102] Wiseman to Laurence, 5 June 1969, in Lennox and Panofsky, eds., *Selected Letters*, 302.

[103] Robert Brow, *The Robert Brow "Model Theology" Webpage: Letters to Surfers*, 27 May 2005, <http://www.brow.on.ca/Letters/reject.htm>.

[104] See Phyllis Grosskurth, *John Addington Symonds: A Biography* (London: Longman, 1964).

[105] Phyllis Grosskurth, personal interview, 28 December 2000.

[106] Ibid.

[107] Wiseman fonds.

[108] Wiseman to Laurence, in Lennox and Panofsky, eds., *Selected Letters*, 309.

[109] Between 11 November 1969 and 2 September 1970, Molinaro also negotiated film rights to *The Sacrifice* with Harry Gulkin of

Productions Kino in Montreal, but Gulkin finally declined a film option on the novel. From 15 June 1961 to 16 January 1963, Willis Kingsley Wing was Wiseman's literary agent. Between 12 March 1969 and 4 October 1973, Wiseman engaged the services of two literary agents: Candida Donadio (from 12 March 1968 to 4 December 1969) and Matie Molinaro (from September 1969 to 4 October 1973). Neither agent was successful in placing *Crackpot*. In general, Wiseman felt that Wing, Donadio, and Molinaro did not represent her authorial interests.

[110] Grosskurth, personal interview.

[111] Ibid.

[112] Freedman, "Stubborn," 28.

[113] Meyer, "Permissable," 126.

[114] Freedman, "Stubborn," 28.

[115] Morisco, "Charm," 141.

[116] Ibid.

[117] Belkin, "Consciousness," 167.

[118] Ibid.

[119] Wiseman to Laurence, 26 May 1973, in Lennox and Panofsky, eds., *Selected Letters*, 335.

[120] Freedman, "Stubborn," 28.

[121] McClelland and Stewart fonds.

[122] Sam Solecki, ed., *Imagining Canadian Literature: The Selected Letters of Jack McClelland* (Toronto: Key Porter Books, 1998), xv.

[123] McClelland to Wiseman, 12 October 1973, McClelland and Stewart fonds.

[124] Wiseman fonds.

[125] McClelland to Wiseman, 29 October 1973, McClelland and Stewart fonds.

[126] Ibid.

[127] McClelland to Wiseman, 16 May 1974, ibid.

[128] Anna Porter to McClelland, 10 December 1973, ibid.

[129] Diane Mew to Linda McKnight, 27 December 1973, ibid.

[130] Wiseman fonds.

[131] McClelland to Wiseman, 25 June 1974, McClelland and Stewart fonds.

[132] [11 or 12 July 1974], ibid.

[133] Wailan Low, 8 July 1974, ibid.

[134] L.T., 11 July 1974, ibid.

[135] Wailan Low, 5 July 1974, ibid.

[136] McClelland and Stewart *Catalogue, 1974*.

[137] Wiseman fonds.

[138] McClelland to Wiseman, 11 September 1974, McClelland and Stewart fonds.

[139] Wiseman fonds.

[140] McClelland to Wiseman, 23 May 1975, McClelland and Stewart fonds.

[141] Bess Kaplan, "*Crackpot*: By Adele Wiseman. A Book Review," *Jewish Post* [Winnipeg], 7 November 1974, p. 7.

[142] Margaret Laurence, "Powerful. Brilliant. The Human Spirit in Fat Whoring Hoda," *Globe and Mail*, 28 September 1974, p. 33.

[143] Barbara Amiel, "Adele Wiseman's Long Layoff Hasn't Altered Her Writing," *Toronto Star*, 21 September 1974, p. F7.

[144] E.G. Mardon, "Book Review: Revolting Second Novel by Wiseman," *Lethbridge Herald*, 12 November 1974.

[145] 2 December 1974.

[146] 28 December 1975.

[147] Ann Crosby, "Books," rev. of *Crackpot*, by Adele Wiseman; and *Season on the Plain*, by Franklin Russell, *Evening Telegram* [St. John's], 25 January 1975, p. 12.

[148] David Legate, "With Unremitting Honesty," *Montreal Star,* 9 November 1974, p. D4.

[149] N.G., "*Crackpot* Bursting with Courage," *Star-Phoenix* [Saskatoon], 8 November 1974, p. 26.

[150] Rev. of *Crackpot*, by Adele Wiseman, *New Westminster* [British Columbia], 26 October 1974.

[151] Robert Weaver, "Readers' Club Selection," *Canadian Reader* 15, 10 [December 1974]: 3.

[152] Geoffrey James, "Canada: Letters. Book of Hoda," *Time* (28 October 1974): 11.

[153] Kendal Windeyer, "Old Hand Tries Again," *Gazette* [Montreal], 5 October 1974, p. 55.

[154] Tom Saunders, "Strange Innocence," *Winnipeg Free Press*, 5 October 1974, p. 20.

[155] George Woodcock, "Books. Adele Wiseman and Sinclair Ross: Return Engagements," rev. of *Sawbones Memorial*, by Sinclair Ross; *Crackpot*, by Adele Wiseman; *Stories from Ontario*, sel. Germaine Warkentin; *Violence in the Arts*, by John Fraser; and *Exxoneration*, by Richard Rohmer, *Maclean's* (October 1974): 110.

[156] Peter Stevens, "Another Novel 18 Years Later," *Windsor Star*, 19 October 1974, p. 14.

[157] Laurence to Wiseman, 12 November 1974, in Lennox and Panofsky, eds., *Selected Letters*, 346.

[158] Weaver, "Readers' Club," 2.

[159] Wachtel, "Profile," 12.

[160] Mack, "What a Woman Can Learn," 135.

[161] Adele Wiseman, *Crackpot* (Toronto: McClelland and Stewart, 1974), 215.

[162] Gillian Lindgren, "Adele Wiseman's Latest Novel Suffers from Verbal Excess," *Herald Magazine* [*Calgary Herald*], 20 December 1974, p. 12.

[163] Ibid.

[164] Margaret Laurence's *The Diviners*, issued in 1974 by McClelland and Stewart, was also criticized for its frank portrayal of female sexuality.

[165] A.J. Arnold, "Literary Comment: Looking at Life from an Off-Beat Locale," *Western Jewish News*, 19 December 1974.

166 See, for example, the following review articles: Russell Brown, "Beyond Sacrifice," *Journal of Canadian Fiction* 16 [1976]: 158-62; Marian Engel, *"Crackpot," Tamarack Review* 65 (March 1975): 91–93; Ken McLean, "Myths Violent and Loving," *Essays on Canadian Writing* 1 (Winter 1974): 56–59; Patricia Monk, rev. of *Crackpot*, by Adele Wiseman, *Quarry* 24, 1 (Winter 1975): 71–72; Helene Rosenthal, "Comedy of Survival," *Canadian Literature* 64 (Spring 1975): 115–18; Kenneth Sherman, *"Crackpot*: A Lurianic Myth," *Waves* 3, 1 (Autumn 1974): 4–11; and Linda Shohet, rev. of *Sawbones Memorial*, by Sinclair Ross; *The Silent Rooms*, by Anne Hébert, trans. Kathy Mezei; and *Crackpot*, by Adele Wiseman, *Canadian Fiction Magazine* 19 (Autumn 1975): 99–102.

167 Rosenthal, "Comedy of Survival," 115.

168 Engel, *"Crackpot,"* 92–93.

169 Bernard Baskin, *"Crackpot* 'Strange, Daring,'" *Spectator* [Hamilton], 28 December 1974, p. 41.

170 See, for example, the following articles: Di Brandt, "That Crazy Wacky Hoda in Winnipeg: A Brief Anatomy of an Honest Attempt at a Pithy Statement about Adele Wiseman's *Crackpot," Prairie Fire* 20, 2 (Summer 1999): 138–47; Michael Greenstein, "The Fissure Queen: Issues of Gender and Post-Colonialism in *Crackpot," Room of One's Own* 16, 3 (September 1993): 20–31; J.M. Kertzer, "Beginnings and Endings: Adele Wiseman's *Crackpot," Essays on Canadian Writing* 58 (Spring 1996): 15–35; Mack, "What a Woman Can Learn," 134–58; Tamara J. Palmer, "Elements of Jewish Culture in Adele Wiseman's *Crackpot*: A Subversive Ethnic Fiction Female Style," *Prairie Forum* 16, 2 (Fall 1991): 265–85; Ruth Panofsky, "From Complicity to Subversion: The Female Subject in Adele Wiseman's Novels," *Canadian Literature* 137 (Summer 1993): 41–50, rpt. in Panofsky, ed., *Adele Wiseman: Essays on Her Works*, Writers Series 7 (Toronto: Guernica Editions, 2001), 55–67; Tamara Palmer Seiler, "Images of Winnipeg's North End: Fictionalizing Space for the Ethnic and Female 'Other,'" in *Woman as Artist: Papers in Honour of Marsh Hanen*, ed. Christine Mason Sutherland and Beverly Matson Rasporich (Calgary: University of Calgary Press, [1993]), 41–69; and Tamara Palmer Seiler, "Including

the Female Immigrant Story: A Comparative Look at Narrative Strategies," *Canadian Ethnic Studies* 28, 1 (1996): 51–66.

[171] Ruth R. Wisse, *The Modern Jewish Canon: A Journey through Language and Culture* (New York: Free Press, 2000), 382.

CHAPTER THREE

[1] See Laura McLauchlan, "The Scrap Toward Knowing in *Old Woman at Play*: Adele Wiseman's Life Writing," *Room of One's Own* 16, 3 (September 1993): 33–40.

[2] Wiseman, *Old Woman*, 6.

[3] Wiseman to Laurence, 26 May 1973, in Lennox and Panofsky, eds., *Selected Letters*, 34.

[4] Wiseman, *Old Woman*, 33.

[5] Wiseman to Laurence, 26 May 1973, in Lennox and Panofsky, eds., *Selected Letters*, 335.

[6] Wiseman to Laurence, 9 [July] 1973, in ibid., 338.

[7] 7 January 1976, in ibid., 348.

[8] Wiseman, *Old Woman*, 126.

[9] Ibid., 39.

[10] McClelland to Linda McKnight, McClelland and Stewart fonds.

[11] McClelland to McKnight, 10 August 1977, ibid.

[12] Ibid.

[13] Jennifer Glossop to McKnight, 12 August 1977, McClelland and Stewart fonds.

[14] Anna Porter to McKnight, 28 September 1977, ibid.

[15] McClelland to Wiseman, 11 October 1977, ibid.

[16] Ibid.

[17] Ibid.

[18] Ibid.

[19] Ibid.

[20] Wiseman to McClelland, 17 May 1978, ibid.

[21] McClelland to Wiseman, 29 May 1978, ibid.

[22] Ibid.

[23] Ibid.

[24] Ibid.

[25] Wiseman to McClelland, 31 May 1978, ibid.

[26] McClelland to Wiseman, 23 January 1980, ibid.

[27] Wiseman, *Memoirs*, 167.

[28] Ibid.

[29] John Pearce, personal interview, 30 July 2002.

[30] Ibid.

[31] Ibid.

[32] Ibid.

[33] Ibid.

[34] Clarke, Irwin fonds.

[35] S.T., Reader's report, 29 November 1977, ibid.

[36] Laurence to John Pearce, 10 December 1977, ibid.

[37] Ibid.

[38] Pearce, personal interview.

[39] S.T., Reader's report, 19 March 1978, Clarke, Irwin fonds.

[40] Pearce, personal interview.

[41] Pearce to Richard Barber, 13 June 1978, Clarke, Irwin fonds.

[42] Wiseman, *Memoirs*, 168.

[43] L.R., rev. of *Old Woman at Play*, by Adele Wiseman, *Alumni Journal* [University of Manitoba] (Autumn 1979): 15.

[44] 28 November 1978, Clarke, Irwin fonds.

[45] Belkin, "Consciousness," 149.

[46] Pearce to Tillie Olsen, 17 January 1979, Clarke, Irwin fonds.

[47] Pearce, personal interview.

[48] Ibid.

[49] Ibid.

[50] Lynne Van Luven, "Books in Review," *Lethbridge Herald*, 23 December 1978, p. 46.

[51] Alison Gordon, "Doll-Maker, Tale-Spinner," *Maclean's* (1 January 1979): 46.

[52] Louise Wyatt, "A Memorable Encounter," *London Free Press*, 16 December 1978, p. B4.

[53] Heather Robertson, "*Old Woman at Play*. Strong-Willed Jewish Mother and Grumpy Daughter: Who Will Win the Power Struggle?" *Globe and Mail*, 17 February 1979, p. 42.

[54] Lynne Van Luven, "Books in Review," p. 46.

[55] Patricia Morley, "Dolls, No Two Alike, Made of Everything," *Ottawa Journal*, 23 December 1978, p. 51.

[56] See Howard Rypp, prod., *Old Woman at Play*, videocassette, Nephesh Theatre, 1983, Wiseman fonds.

[57] Pearce, personal interview.

[58] Richard Teleky, personal interview, 4 June 2001.

[59] Ibid. The series included the following titles: Linda Hutcheon's *The Canadian Postmodern: A Study of Contemporary English-Canadian Fiction* (1988) and *Splitting Images: Contemporary Canadian Ironies* (1991); Janice Kulyk Keefer's *Reading Mavis Gallant* (1989); Robert Kroetsch's *The Lovely Treachery of Words: Essays Selected and New* (1989); Miriam Waddington's *Apartment Seven: Essays Selected and New* (1989); and Adele Wiseman's *Memoirs of a Book Molesting Childhood and Other Essays* (1987).

[60] Teleky, personal interview.

[61] Several of the essays had appeared in *Canadian Forum*; *Chinada: Memoirs of the Gang of Seven*; *International Journal of Women's Studies*; *Journal of Canadian Studies*; and *Old Markets, New World*.

[62] Teleky, personal interview.

[63] Ibid.

[64] Ibid. See "What Price the Heroine?" in *Memoirs of a Book Molesting Childhood and Other Essays* (Toronto: Oxford University Press, 1987), 63–80.

65 Ken Adachi, "Wiseman Wrote a Moving Memoir," *Sunday Star* [Toronto], 15 November 1987, p. A23.

66 Elizabeth Greene, "On Aiming for the Highest," *Whig-Standard Magazine* [Kingston], 19 December 1987, p. 27.

67 Sharon Drache, "Book Review," *Ottawa Jewish Bulletin and Review*, 4 March 1988, p. 21.

68 Adachi, "Wiseman Wrote," p. A23.

69 Glenn Deer, "Heroic Artists," rev. of *Margaret Atwood*, by Barbara Hill Rigney; *Emily Carr*, by Ruth Gowers; and *Memoirs of a Book Molesting Childhood and Other Essays*, by Adele Wiseman, *Canadian Literature* 120 (Spring 1989): 152.

70 Marion K. Quednau, "Those Accidents of Truth that Sneak Up," *Globe and Mail*, 26 December 1987, p. C23.

71 Teleky, personal interview.

72 Ibid.

73 Ibid. Teleky now heads the Creative Writing Program at Toronto's York University. He is the author of *Goodnight, Sweetheart and Other Stories* (1993); *Hungarian Rhapsodies: Essays on Ethnicity, Identity, and Culture* (1997); *The Paris Years of Rosie Kamin* (1998); and *Pack Up the Moon* (2001).

74 Teleky, personal interview.

75 Harry Gutkin, *The Worst of Times, The Best of Times* (Markham: Fitzhenry and Whiteside, 1987), 205–06.

CHAPTER FOUR

1 Lazar, "Mentorship," 25.

2 Ibid., 28.

3 Elizabeth A. Meese, "Archival Materials: The Problem of Literary Reputation," in *Opportunities for Women's Studies Publication Research in Language and Literature*, ed. Joan E. Hartman and Ellen Messer-Davidow, Women in Print 1 (New York: Modern Language Association, 1983), 39.

4 Russell Brown, rev. of *Selected Letters of Margaret Laurence and Adele Wiseman*, ed. John Lennox and Ruth Panofsky; and *We Who Can Fly:*

Poems, Essays and Memories in Honour of Adele Wiseman, ed. Elizabeth Greene, *University of Toronto Quarterly* 68, 1 (Winter 1998–99): 569.

[5] Sylvia Fraser, "II: Remembering Adele," in *We Who Can Fly: Poems, Essays and Memories in Honour of Adele Wiseman*, ed. Elizabeth Greene (Dunvegan: Cormorant Books, 1997), 14.

[6] Lazar, "Mentorship," 25.

[7] Adele Wiseman, "Pooh at Puberty," rev. of *Bear*, by Marian Engel, *Books in Canada* (April 1976): 6.

[8] Adele Wiseman, "Readers Can Rejoice Atwood's in Form," rev. of *Life before Man*, by Margaret Atwood, *Toronto Star*, 29 September 1979, p. F7.

[9] Adele Wiseman, "Ukrainians' History Painfully Recreated," rev. of *All of Baba's Children*, by Myrna Kostash, *Toronto Star*, 24 December 1977, p. D7.

[10] Adele Wiseman, "Peeling Away All the Layers of a Zany Life," rev. of *Basic Black with Pearls*, by Helen Weinzweig, *Toronto Star*, 17 May 1980, p. E9.

[11] Adele Wiseman, "Drunken Hero Fails His Modern Cinderella," rev. of *A Casual Affair: A Modern Fairytale*, by Sylvia Fraser, *Toronto Star*, 11 March 1978, p. D7.

[12] Fraser, "Remembering Adele," 13.

[13] See Kenneth Sherman, "*Crackpot*: A Lurianic Myth," *Waves* 3, 1 (Autumn 1974): 4–11.

[14] Kenneth Sherman, personal interview, 7 July 2000.

[15] Anne Michaels, "The Hooded Hawk," in *We Who Can Fly: Poems, Essays and Memories in Honour of Adele Wiseman*, ed. Elizabeth Greene (Dunvegan: Cormorant Books, 1997), 38.

[16] Janis Rapoport, personal interview, 3 May 2001.

[17] Sharon Drache, personal interview, 6 February 2001.

[18] Digges, "Waiting Room," 112.

[19] Ibid.

[20] Wiseman to McClelland, 15 November 1975, McClelland and Stewart fonds.

21 Wiseman, *Memoirs*, 96.

22 Ibid., 106.

23 Sheila Robinson Fallis, "Writer-in-Residence Adele Wiseman 'Is Warmth Itself,'" *University of Toronto Graduate* (Winter 1976): 4.

24 Grosskurth, personal interview.

25 Fallis, "Writer-in-Residence," 4.

26 Lou Seligson, "Writer-in-Residence Tries to Make a Better World," *Canadian Jewish News* [Montreal edition], 2 February 1984, p. 13.

27 Sheila Robinson Fallis, "'Writers Are Just People Who Work at Writing,'" *University of Toronto Bulletin*, 12 September 1975, p. 6.

28 Lenore Langs, "Adele as Poet and Inspirer of Poetry," in *We Who Can Fly: Poems, Essays and Memories in Honour of Adele Wiseman*, ed. Elizabeth Greene (Dunvegan: Cormorant Books, 1997), 120.

29 Ingrid MacDonald, "Untitled," in *We Who Can Fly: Poems, Essays and Memories in Honour of Adele Wiseman*, ed. Elizabeth Greene (Dunvegan: Cormorant Books, 1997), 31.

30 Don Coles, "Adele at Banff," in *We Who Can Fly: Poems, Essays and Memories in Honour of Adele Wiseman*, ed. Elizabeth Greene (Dunvegan: Cormorant Books, 1997), 67.

31 Caroline Adderson, "Wingless, Fearless," in *We Who Can Fly: Poems, Essays and Memories in Honour of Adele Wiseman*, ed. Elizabeth Greene (Dunvegan: Cormorant Books, 1997), 71.

32 Stella Body, "Red Hat," in *We Who Can Fly: Poems, Essays and Memories in Honour of Adele Wiseman*, ed. Elizabeth Greene (Dunvegan: Cormorant Books, 1997), 76.

33 Ibid.

34 [Elizabeth Greene], "Interview with Steven Heighton and Mary Cameron," in *We Who Can Fly: Poems, Essays and Memories in Honour of Adele Wiseman*, ed. Greene (Dunvegan: Cormorant Books, 1997), 83.

35 Ibid., 81.

36 Ibid., 86.

[37] Colin Bernhardt, "Untitled," in *We Who Can Fly: Poems, Essays and Memories in Honour of Adele Wiseman*, ed. Elizabeth Greene (Dunvegan: Cormorant Books, 1997), 96.

[38] Ven Begamudré, "Adele Here, Not Here," in *We Who Can Fly: Poems, Essays and Memories in Honour of Adele Wiseman*, ed. Elizabeth Greene (Dunvegan: Cormorant Books, 1997), 92.

[39] Evelyn McLean, "Wiseman on Words," *University of Windsor Alumni Magazine* 9, 1 (Spring 1989): 27.

[40] Body, "Red Hat," 75.

[41] Ibid.

[42] Ibid.

[43] Elizabeth Greene, Introduction, in *We Who Can Fly: Poems, Essays and Memories in Honour of Adele Wiseman*, ed. Greene (Dunvegan: Cormorant Books, 1997), xvi.

[44] Lazar, "Mentorship," 32.

[45] Ibid., 25.

[46] Adele Wiseman, "Marian Engel 1933–1985," *Canadian Literature* 108 (Spring 1986): 198–99.

[47] Elizabeth Greene, "Remembering Adele Wiseman (May 21, 1928–June 1, 1992)," *Whig-Standard Magazine* [Kingston], 4 July 1992, p. 19.

[48] Janis Rapoport, "Remembering Adele Wiseman," *Toronto Star*, 6 June 1992, p. G6.

[49] The following individuals participated in the memorial tribute to Adele Wiseman: Arlene Lampert (long-time friend); Jocelyn Laurence (Margaret and Jack Laurence's daughter); David Laurence (Margaret and Jack Laurence's son); Sylvia Fraser (friend and writer); Phyllis Grosskurth (friend and writer); Janis Rapoport (friend and writer); Joyce Marshall (friend and writer); Anne Michaels (friend and writer); Ingrid MacDonald (student, friend, and writer); Rachel Wyatt (friend and writer); Sidney and Mary Perlmutter (lifelong friends); and Tamara Stone (Adele Wiseman and Dmitry Stone's daughter). See Christina Kurata, dir., *Tribute to Adele Wiseman*, videocassette, 10 May 1993, Wiseman fonds.

[50] Linda Rogers, *The Broad Canvas: Portraits of Women* (Victoria: Sono Nis Press, 1999), 73.

[51] Qtd. in ibid., 73.

[52] Ibid.

[53] Jack Ruttan, "Re: Canada Reads," online posting, 18 April 2002, Canlit-l, 18 April 2002, <http://www.nld-bnc.ca/6/20/s20-230-e.html>.

[54] Rogers, *Broad*, 72, 76.

[55] McLauchlan, "Scrap Toward Knowing," 33.

[56] Donna Bennett, "'Let me get it right': Adele Wiseman as Essayist," in *Adele Wiseman: Essays on Her Works*, ed. Ruth Panofsky, Writers Series 7 (Toronto: Guernica Editions, 2001), 121.

[57] Judith Fitzgerald, "Bite," *Globe and Mail*, 30 October 1999, p. D30.

[58] Robert Adams, *A Love of Reading: Reviews of Contemporary Fiction* (Toronto: McClelland and Stewart, 2001), 304.

[59] Seymour Mayne, "That Third Big Fiction," in *We Who Can Fly: Poems, Essays and Memories in Honour of Adele Wiseman*, ed. Elizabeth Greene (Dunvegan: Cormorant Books, 1997), 175.

[60] Wiseman, "Marian Engel," 200.

[61] Wiseman, "Pooh," 6. The existence of unpublished Wiseman manuscripts (essays, children's stories, and poems) in the Adele Wiseman fonds, Clara Thomas Archives, Scott Library, York University, holds the promise of posthumous publication.

A) PRIMARY SOURCES

Archival Collections

Canadian Speakers' and Writers' Service Ltd. fonds. F0280, folder 1984–006/010(01); folder 1985–008/013(02). Clara Thomas Archives, Scott Library, York University.

Clarke, Irwin and Company Limited fonds. William Ready Division of Archives and Research Collections, McMaster University Library.

Curtis Brown Ltd. archives. MsColl/Curtis Brown, box 485; box 1078; box 1348, folder 5. Rare Book and Manuscript Library, Columbia University.

Gray, John Morgan. John Morgan Gray fonds. MG30-D266. Library and Archives Canada.

Laurence, Margaret. Margaret Laurence fonds. F0341. Clara Thomas Archives, Scott Library, York University.

Macmillan Company of Canada fonds. Author correspondence, box 141, folder 6: *The Sacrifice* 1955–71; box 281, folder 1: *Crackpot* 1965–69. William Ready Division of Archives and Research Collections, McMaster University Library.

McClelland, Jack. Jack McClelland fonds. William Ready Division of Archives and Research Collections, McMaster University Library.

McClelland and Stewart Ltd. fonds. Boxes 101; CC56; CP1; JP15; JP31; TR18: *Crackpot* 1973–78. William Ready Division of Archives and Research Collections, McMaster University Library.

The Reminiscences of Marshall Ayres Best (1976). Oral History Research Collection, Rare Book and Manuscript Library, Columbia University. Transcript.

Ross, Malcolm. Malcolm Ross fonds. MsC 18. Special Collections, University of Calgary Library.

___. Malcolm Ross papers. MS Coll 00277. Thomas Fisher Rare Book Library, University of Toronto.

Weaver, Robert. Robert Weaver fonds. MG31–D162, vol. 5, folder 27; vol. 13, folder 197. Library and Archives Canada.

Wiseman, Adele. Adele Wiseman fonds. F0447. Clara Thomas Archives, Scott Library, York University.

Interviews

Dobbs, Kildare. Personal interview. 8 November 1999.

Dorn, Miriam. Personal interview. 21 April 2001.

Drache, Sharon. Personal interview. 6 February 2001.

Grosskurth, Phyllis. Personal interview. 28 December 2000.

Kurata, Christina. Personal interview. 21 June 2001.

Pearce, John. Personal interview. 30 July 2002.

Perlmutter, Sidney. Personal interview. 1 December 1999.

Rapoport, Janis. Personal interview. 3 May 2001.

Richler, Mordecai. Personal interview. 19 November 1999.

Rosenfarb, Chava. Personal interview. 25 October 2000.

Ross, Malcolm. Telephone interview. 14 October 1999.

Sherman, Kenneth. Personal interview. 7 July 2000.

Speers, John. Personal interview. 11 November 1999.

Teleky, Richard. Personal interview. 4 June 2001.

Weaver, Robert. Personal interview. 6 April 2000.

B) SECONDARY SOURCES

Adachi, Ken. "Wiseman Wrote a Moving Memoir." *Sunday Star* [Toronto], 15 November 1987, p. A23.

Adams, Richard. *Watership Down*. London: Rex Collings, 1972.

Adams, Robert. *A Love of Reading: Reviews of Contemporary Fiction*. Toronto: McClelland and Stewart, 2001.

Adderson, Caroline. "Wingless, Fearless." In *We Who Can Fly: Poems, Essays and Memories in Honour of Adele Wiseman*. Ed. Elizabeth Greene. Dunvegan: Cormorant Books, 1997, 69–71.

Amiel, Barbara. "Adele Wiseman's Long Layoff Hasn't Altered Her Writing." *Toronto Star*, 21 September 1974, p. F7.

Arnold, A.J. "Literary Comment: Looking at Life from an Off-Beat Locale." *Western Jewish News*, 19 December 1974.

Atwood, Margaret. *Life before Man*. Toronto: McClelland and Stewart, 1979.

Baskin, Bernard. "*Crackpot* 'Strange, Daring.'" *Spectator* [Hamilton], 28 December 1974, p. 41.

Begamudré, Ven. "Adele Here, Not Here." In *We Who Can Fly: Poems, Essays and Memories in Honour of Adele Wiseman*. Ed. Elizabeth Greene. Dunvegan: Cormorant Books, 1997, 91–94.

Belkin, Roslyn. "The Consciousness of a Jewish Artist: An Interview with Adele Wiseman." *Journal of Canadian Fiction* 31–32 (1981): 148–76.

Bennett, Donna. "'Let me get it right': Adele Wiseman as Essayist." In *Adele Wiseman: Essays on Her Works*. Ed. Ruth Panofsky. Writers Series 7. Toronto: Guernica Editions, 2001, 105–22.

Bennett, Edgar. Rev. of *Crackpot*, by Adele Wiseman. CBC Radio. Halifax. 2 December 1974. Transcript.

Bernhardt, Colin. "Untitled." In *We Who Can Fly: Poems, Essays and Memories in Honour of Adele Wiseman*. Ed. Elizabeth Greene. Dunvegan: Cormorant Books, 1997, 95–96.

Body, Stella. "Red Hat." In *We Who Can Fly: Poems, Essays and Memories in Honour of Adele Wiseman*. Ed. Elizabeth Greene. Dunvegan: Cormorant Books, 1997, 72–79.

Brotten, Delores, and Peter Birdsall. *Paper Phoenix: A History of Book Publishing in English Canada*. Victoria: Canlit, 1980.

Brow, Robert. *The Robert Brow "Model Theology" Webpage: Letters to Surfers*. 27 May 2005. <http://www.brow.on.ca/Letters/reject.htm>.

Brown, Russell. "Beyond Sacrifice." *Journal of Canadian Fiction* 16 [1976]: 158–62.

___. Rev. of *Selected Letters of Margaret Laurence and Adele Wiseman*, ed. John Lennox and Ruth Panofsky; and *We Who Can Fly: Poems, Essays and Memories in Honour of Adele Wiseman*, ed. Elizabeth Greene. *University of Toronto Quarterly* 68, 1 (Winter 1998–99): 566–70.

Butovsky, Mervin. "Interview with Adele Wiseman." *Room of One's Own* 16, 3 (September 1993): 5–14.

Cameron, Elspeth. *Earle Birney: A Life*. Toronto: Viking Press, 1994.

Chittick, Kathryn. "*SCL* Interviews: Malcolm Ross." *Studies in Canadian Literature* 9, 2 (Summer 1984): 241–66.

Cohen, Leonard. *Beautiful Losers*. Toronto: McClelland and Stewart, 1966.

Cohen, Matt. *The Disinherited*. Toronto: McClelland and Stewart, 1974.

Coles, Don. "Adele at Banff." In *We Who Can Fly: Poems, Essays and Memories in Honour of Adele Wiseman*. Ed. Elizabeth Greene. Dunvegan: Cormorant Books, 1997, 65–69.

Creighton, Sally. Rev. of *The Sacrifice*, by Adele Wiseman. *Critically Speaking*. CBC Radio, Vancouver. 30 September 1956. Transcript.

Crosby, Ann. "Books." Rev. of *Crackpot*, by Adele Wiseman; and *Season on the Plain*, by Franklin Russell. *Evening Telegram* [St. John's], 25 January 1975, p. 12.

Davey, Frank. "Writers and Publishers in English-Canadian Literature." In F. Davey, *Reading Canadian Reading*. Winnipeg: Turnstone Press, 1988, 87–103.

DeCook, Travis. "The History of the Book, Literary History, and Identity Politics in Canada." *Studies in Canadian Literature* 27, 2 (2002): 71–87.

Deer, Glenn. "Heroic Artists." Rev. of *Margaret Atwood*, by Barbara Hill Rigney; *Emily Carr*, by Ruth Gowers; and *Memoirs of a Book Molesting Childhood and Other Essays*, by Adele Wiseman. *Canadian Literature* 120 (Spring 1989): 150–53.

Dickson, Lovat. "Gray, John Morgan." In *The Oxford Companion to Canadian Literature*. Second edition. Ed. Eugene Benson and William Toye. Toronto: Oxford University Press, 1997, 492.

Digges, Deborah. "The Waiting Room Door." *Ohio Review* 51 (1994): 112–19.

Donovan, Josephine. "Toward a Women's Poetics." In *Feminist Issues in Literary Scholarship*. Ed. Shari Benstock. Bloomington: Indiana University Press, 1987, 100.

Drache, Sharon. "Book Review." *Ottawa Jewish Bulletin and Review*, 4 March 1988, p. 21.

Edwards, Ruth Dudley. *Victor Gollancz: A Biography*. London: Victor Gollancz, 1987.

Eliot, T.S. *The Cocktail Party: A Comedy*. London: Faber and Faber, 1950.

Engel, Howard. "Dobbs, Kildare." In *The Oxford Companion to Canadian Literature*. Second edition. Ed. Eugene Benson and William Toye. Toronto: Oxford University Press, 1997, 297–98.

Engel, Marian. *Bear*. Toronto: McClelland and Stewart, 1976.

____. "Crackpot." *Tamarack Review* 65 (March 1975): 91–93.

Fallis, Sheila Robinson. "Writer-in-Residence Adele Wiseman 'Is Warmth Itself.'" *University of Toronto Graduate* (Winter 1976): 4+.

____. "'Writers Are Just People Who Work at Writing.'" *University of Toronto Bulletin*, 12 September 1975, p. 6.

Findley, Timothy. *The Wars*. Toronto: Clarke, Irwin, 1977.

Fitzgerald, Judith. "Bite." *Globe and Mail*, 30 October 1999, p. D30.

Fleming, Patricia Lockhart, and Yvan Lamonde, gen. eds. *History of the Book in Canada*. Three volumes. Toronto: University of Toronto Press, 2004–2007.

Fraser, Sylvia. *A Casual Affair: A Modern Fairytale*. Toronto: McClelland and Stewart, 1978.

___. "II: Remembering Adele." In *We Who Can Fly: Poems, Essays and Memories in Honour of Adele Wiseman*. Ed. Elizabeth Greene. Dunvegan: Cormorant Books, 1997, 13–15.

Freedman, Adele. "The Stubborn Ethnicity of Adele W." *Saturday Night* (May 1976): 23–28.

Fulford, Robert. "But Why Own It?" Rev. of Canada, photog. Peter Varley, intro. Kildare Dobbs; and Old Markets, New World, text Adele Wiseman, illus. Joe Rosenthal. *Toronto Daily Star*, 21 November 1964, p. 26.

G., N. "*Crackpot* Bursting with Courage." *Star-Phoenix* [Saskatoon], 8 November 1974, p. 26.

G[elman], J[oe] M. "A Saturday Review: New Books and Old. Greatness Achieved." *Winnipeg Free Press*, 29 September 1956, p. 9.

George, Diana Hume. "A Vision of My Obscured Soul." *Ohio Review* 51 (1994): 41–52.

Gerson, Carole. "The Canadian Publishers' Records Database and Canadian Book History." Address. Bibliographical Society of Canada, 28 June 2004.

___. "The Canon between the Wars: Field-Notes of a Feminist Literary Archaeologist." In *Canadian Canons: Essays in Literary Value*. Ed. Robert Lecker. Toronto: University of Toronto Press, 1991, 46–56.

Givner, Joan. *Mazo de la Roche: The Hidden Life*. Toronto: Oxford University Press, 1998.

Gordon, Alison. "Doll-Maker, Tale-Spinner." *Maclean's* (1 January 1979): 46.

Grant, Judith Skelton. *Robertson Davies: Man of Myth*. Toronto: Viking Press, 1994.

Gray, John Morgan. *A.W. Mackenzie, The Grove, Lakefield: A Memoir*. Toronto: Grove Old Boys' Association, 1938.

___. "Canadian Books: A Publisher's View." *Canadian Literature* 33 (Summer 1967): 25–36.

___. *Fun Tomorrow: Learning to Be a Publisher and Much Else*. Toronto: Macmillan, 1978.

___. *Lord Selkirk of Red River*. Toronto: Macmillan, 1963.

___. *The One-Eyed Trapper*. Toronto: Macmillan, 1942.

___, and Frank A. Upjohn, eds. *Prose of Our Day*. Toronto: Macmillan, 1940.

Green, Elizabeth. Introduction. In *We Who Can Fly: Poems, Essays and Memories in Honour of Adele Wiseman*. Ed. E. Greene. Dunvegan: Cormorant Books, 1997, xiii–xxvii.

___. "On Aiming for the Highest." *Whig-Standard Magazine* [Kingston], 19 December 1987, p. 27.

___. "Remembering Adele Wiseman (May 21, 1928–June 1, 1992)." *Whig-Standard Magazine* [Kingston], 4 July 1992, p. 19.

___. "Interview with Steven Heighton and Mary Cameron." In *We Who Can Fly: Poems, Essays and Memories in Honour of Adele Wiseman*. Ed. E. Greene. Dunvegan: Cormorant Books, 1997, 80–90.

Greene, Hannah. *I Never Promised You a Rose Garden*. New York: Holt, Rinehart and Winston, 1964.

Greenstein, Michael. "The Fissure Queen: Issues of Gender and Post-Colonialism in *Crackpot*." *Room of One's Own* 16, 3 (September 1993): 20–31.

Grescoe, Paul. *The Merchants of Venus: Inside Harlequin and the Empire of Romance*. Vancouver: Raincoast Books, 1996.

Grosskurth, Phyllis. *John Addington Symonds: A Biography*. London: Longman, 1964.

Gutkin, Harry. *The Worst of Times, The Best of Times*. Markham: Fitzhenry and Whiteside, 1987.

Halpenny, Francess. "Bibliography: The Foundation of Scholarship." In *Symposium on Scholarly Communication: Papers Delivered at the Symposium Held in Ottawa in October 1980.* Ottawa: Aid to Scholarly Publications Programme, 1981, 41–49.

____. "From Author to Reader." In *Literary History of Canada.* Second edition. Volume 4. Gen. ed. W.H. New. Toronto: University of Toronto Press, 1990, 385–404.

Hutcheon, Linda. *The Canadian Postmodern: A Study of Contemporary English-Canadian Fiction.* Studies in Canadian Literature. Toronto: Oxford University Press, 1988.

____. *Splitting Images: Contemporary Canadian Ironies.* Studies in Canadian Literature. Toronto: Oxford University Press, 1991.

James, Geoffrey. "Canada: Letters. Book of Hoda." *Time* (28 October 1974): 11.

James, Henry. *The Portrait of a Lady.* London: Macmillan, 1881.

Kaplan, Bess. "*Crackpot*: By Adele Wiseman. A Book Review." *Jewish Post* [Winnipeg], 7 November 1974, p. 7.

Karr, Clarence. *Authors and Audiences: Popular Canadian Fiction in the Early Twentieth Century.* Montreal: McGill-Queen's University Press, 2000.

Keefer, Janice Kulyk. *Reading Mavis Gallant.* Studies in Canadian Literature. Toronto: Oxford University Press, 1989.

Kertzer, J.M. "Beginnings and Endings: Adele Wiseman's *Crackpot*." *Essays on Canadian Writing* 58 (Spring 1996): 15–35.

King, James. *Farley: The Life of Farley Mowat.* Toronto: HarperFlamingoCanada, 2002.

____. *Jack, A Life with Writers: The Story of Jack McClelland.* Toronto: Alfred A. Knopf Canada, 1999.

____. *The Life of Margaret Laurence.* Toronto: Alfred A. Knopf Canada, 1997.

Kostash, Myrna. *All of Baba's Children.* Edmonton: Hurtig Publishers, 1977.

Kreisel, Henry. *The Rich Man.* Toronto: McClelland and Stewart, 1948.

Kroetsch, Robert. *The Lovely Treachery of Words: Essays Selected and New.* Studies in Canadian Literature. Toronto: Oxford University Press, 1989.

Kurata, Christina, dir. *Tribute to Adele Wiseman.* Videocassette. 10 May 1993. Adele Wiseman fonds. Clara Thomas Archives, Scott Library, York University.

Langs, Lenore. "Adele as Poet and Inspirer of Poetry." In *We Who Can Fly: Poems, Essays and Memories in Honour of Adele Wiseman.* Ed. Elizabeth Greene. Dunvegan: Cormorant Books, 1997, 113–23.

Laurence, Margaret. *Dance on the Earth: A Memoir.* Toronto: McClelland and Stewart, 1989.

____. *The Diviners.* London: Macmillan, 1974.

____. *The Fire-Dwellers.* London: Macmillan, 1969.

____. "Powerful. Brilliant. The Human Spirit in Fat Whoring Hoda." *Globe and Mail,* 28 September 1974, p. 33.

____. *The Stone Angel.* London: Macmillan, 1964.

____. *This Side Jordan.* London: Macmillan, 1960.

Lazar, David. "On Mentorship." *Ohio Review* 51 (1994): 25–33.

Legate, David. "With Unremitting Honesty." *Montreal Star,* 9 November 1974, p. D4.

Lennox, John, and Ruth Panofsky, eds. *Selected Letters of Margaret Laurence and Adele Wiseman.* Toronto: University of Toronto Press, 1997.

Lindgren, Gillian. "Adele Wiseman's Latest Novel Suffers from Verbal Excess." *Herald Magazine* [*Calgary Herald*], 20 December 1974, p. 12.

MacDonald, Ingrid. "Untitled." In *We Who Can Fly: Poems, Essays and Memories in Honour of Adele Wiseman.* Ed. Elizabeth Greene. Dunvegan: Cormorant Books, 1997, 31–33.

Mack, Marcia. "*The Sacrifice* and *Crackpot*: What a Woman Can Learn by Rewriting a Fairy Tale and Clarifying Its Meaning." *Essays on Canadian Writing* 68 (Summer 1999): 134–58.

MacSkimming, Roy. *Making Literary History: House of Anansi Press 1967–1997*. Concord: House of Anansi Press, 1997.

___. *The Perilous Trade: Publishing Canada's Writers*. Toronto: McClelland and Stewart, 2003.

Maloff, Saul. "Books and Comment: The World of Double Exile." *New Republic*, 12 November 1956, pp. 20–21.

Mardon, E.G. "Book Review: Revolting Second Novel by Wiseman." *Lethbridge Herald*, 12 November 1974.

Mayne, Seymour. "That Third Big Fiction." In *We Who Can Fly: Poems, Essays and Memories in Honour of Adele Wiseman*. Ed. Elizabeth Greene. Dunvegan: Cormorant Books, 1997, 175.

McCaig, JoAnn. *Reading in Alice Munro's Archives*. Waterloo: Wilfrid Laurier University Press, 2002.

McClelland and Stewart. *Catalogue*. 1974.

McKenna, Isobel. *The Bookshelf: Ottawa Public Library Sunday Radio Review*. CFMO, CFRA, CJET Ottawa. 28 December 1975. Transcript.

McLauchlan, Laura. "The Scrap Toward Knowing in *Old Woman at Play*: Adele Wiseman's Life Writing." *Room of One's Own* 16, 3 (September 1993): 33–40.

McLean, Evelyn. "Wiseman on Words." *University of Windsor Alumni Magazine* 9, 1 (Spring 1989): 24–27.

McLean, Ken. "Myths Violent and Loving." *Essays on Canadian Writing* 1 (Winter 1974): 56–59.

Meese, Elizabeth A. "Archival Materials: The Problem of Literary Reputation." *Opportunities for Women's Studies Publication Research in Language and Literature*. Ed. Joan E. Hartman and Ellen Messer-Davidow. Women in Print 1. New York: Modern Language Association, 1982, 37–46.

Meyer, Bruce, and Brian O'Riordan. "The Permissible and the Possible: Adele Wiseman." In *Lives and Works: Interviews*. Windsor: Black Moss Press, 1992, 118–27.

Michaels, Anne. "The Hooded Hawk." In *We Who Can Fly: Poems, Essays and Memories in Honour of Adele Wiseman.* Ed. Elizabeth Greene. Dunvegan: Cormorant Books, 1997, 34–38.

Mitchell, M.M. "Saturday Review of Books: Ukrainian Jews Try New Life in Winnipeg." *Globe and Mail,* 6 October 1956, p. 5.

Monk, Patricia. Rev. of *Crackpot,* by Adele Wiseman. *Quarry* 24, 1 (Winter 1975): 71–72.

Morley, Patricia. "Dolls, No Two Alike, Made of Everything." *Ottawa Journal,* 23 December 1978, p. 51.

Morisco, Gabriella. "The Charm of an Unorthodox Feminism: An Interview with Adele Wiseman." In *We Who Can Fly: Poems, Essays and Memories in Honour of Adele Wiseman.* Ed. Elizabeth Greene. Dunvegan: Cormorant Books, 1997, 125–46.

Mount, Nick. *When Canadian Literature Moved to New York.* Toronto: University of Toronto Press, 2005.

Munro, Alice. *Something I've Been Meaning to Tell You.* Toronto: McGraw-Hill Ryerson, 1974.

Nadel, Ira B. *Various Positions: A Life of Leonard Cohen.* Toronto: Random House of Canada, 1996.

New, W.H. *A History of Canadian Literature.* Montreal: McGill-Queen's University Press, 1989.

"New Fiction." Rev. of *Destination Berlin,* by Paul Vialar, trans. Philip John Stead; *The Sacrifice,* by Adele Wiseman; *Splendid Sunday,* by James Ambrose Brown; *The Last Resort,* by Pamela Hansford Johnson; and *Ferguson,* by Rayne Kruger. *Times* [London], 8 November 1956, p. 13.

Palmer, Tamara J. "Elements of Jewish Culture in Adele Wiseman's *Crackpot*: A Subversive Ethnic Fiction Female Style." *Prairie Forum* 16, 2 (Fall 1991): 265–85.

Panofsky, Ruth. "From Complicity to Subversion: The Female Subject in Adele Wiseman's Novels." *Canadian Literature* 137 (Summer 1993): 41–48. Rpt. in *Adele Wiseman: Essays on Her Works.* Ed. R. Panofsky. Writers Series 7. Toronto: Guernica Editions, 2001, 55–67.

____. "'Sister Friend': The Correspondence of Margaret Laurence and Adele Wiseman." *Room of One's Own* 16, 3 (September 1993): 58–67.

____. "Sketches from the Life: A Log." In *We Who Can Fly: Poems, Essays and Memories in Honour of Adele Wiseman.* Ed. Elizabeth Greene. Dunvegan: Cormorant Books, 1997, 253–66.

____. "Success Well-Earned: Adele Wiseman's *The Sacrifice.*" *English Studies in Canada* 27, 3 (September 2001): 333–51.

____, and Michael Moir. "Halted by the Archive: The Impact of Excessive Archival Restrictions on Scholars." *Journal of Scholarly Publishing* 37, 1 (October 2005): 19–32.

____, ed. *Adele Wiseman: Essays on Her Works.* Writers Series 7. Toronto: Guernica Editions, 2001.

Prescott, Orville. "Books of The Times." *New York Times,* 14 September 1956, p. 21.

Quednau, Marion K. "Those Accidents of Truth that Sneak Up." *Globe and Mail,* 26 December 1987, p. C23.

R. L. Rev. of *Old Woman at Play,* by Adele Wiseman. *Alumni Journal* [University of Manitoba] (Autumn 1979): 15.

Rapoport, Janis. "Remembering Adele Wiseman." *Toronto Star,* 6 June 1992, p. G6.

Rev. of *Crackpot,* by Adele Wiseman. *New Westminster* [British Columbia], 26 October 1974.

Ricard, François. *Gabrielle Roy, une vie: biographie.* Montréal: Boréal, 1996.

Rich, Adrienne. *On Lies, Secrets, and Silences: Selected Prose 1966–1978.* New York: Norton, 1979.

Richardson, Jean. "Gollancz: The House that Victor Built." *British Book News* (June 1989): 396–99.

Richler, Mordecai. *Son of a Smaller Hero.* London: Andre Deutsch, 1955.

Robertson, Heather. "*Old Woman at Play.* Strong-Willed Jewish Mother and Grumpy Daughter: Who Will Win the Power Struggle?" *Globe and Mail,* 17 February 1979, p. 42.

Rogers, Linda. *The Broad Canvas: Portraits of Women.* Victoria: Sono Nis Press, 1999.

Rosenthal, Helene. "Comedy of Survival." *Canadian Literature* 64 (Spring 1975): 115–18.

Ross, Sinclair. *Sawbones Memorial.* Toronto: McClelland and Stewart, 1974.

Ruttan, Jack. "Re: Canada Reads." Online posting. 18 April 2002. Canlit-l. 18 April 2002. <http://www.nlc-bnc.ca/6/20/s20-230-e.html>.

Rypp, Howard, prod. *Old Woman at Play.* Videocassette. Nephesh Theatre, 1983. Adele Wiseman fonds. Clara Thomas Archives, Scott Library, York University.

Sabbath, Lawrence. "New Outlook to an Old Tradition." *Gazette* [Montreal], 29 September 1956, p. 31.

Saunders, Tom. "Strange Innocence." *Winnipeg Free Press*, 5 October 1974, p. 20.

Scott, Gail. *Spaces like stairs.* Toronto: Women's Press, 1989.

Scott, James. "The Abraham Story: New Author Rises on Canadian Scene." *Telegram* [Toronto], 15 September 1956, p. 34.

Scott, Winfield Townley. "Modern Scene, Biblical Echoes in a Fine, Mature First Novel." *New York Herald Tribune*, 16 September 1956, sec. 5, p. 1.

Seiler, Tamara Palmer. "Images of Winnipeg's North End: Fictionalizing Space for the Ethnic and Female 'Other.'" In *Woman as Artist: Papers in Honour of Marsh Hanen.* Ed. Christine Mason Sutherland and Beverly Matson Rasporich. Calgary: University of Calgary Press, [1993], 41–69.

___. "Including the Female Immigrant Story: A Comparative Look at Narrative Strategies." *Canadian Ethnic Studies* 28, 1 (1996): 51–66.

Seligson, Lou. "Writer-in-Residence Tries to Make a Better World." *Canadian Jewish News* [Montreal edition], 2 February 1984, p. 13.

Sherman, Kenneth. "*Crackpot*: A Lurianic Myth." *Waves* 3, 1 (Autumn 1974): 4–11.

Shields, Carol. "Brave Bulletins from the Mother Zone." Rev. of *The Mother Zone: Love, Sex and Laundry in the Modern Family*, by Marni Jackson. *Globe and Mail*, 7 October 1992, p. C24.

Shohet, Linda. Rev. of *Sawbones Memorial*, by Sinclair Ross; *The Silent Rooms*, by Anne Hébert, trans. Kathy Mezei; and *Crackpot*, by Adele Wiseman. *Canadian Fiction Magazine* 19 (Autumn 1975): 99–102.

Slopen, Beverley. "Malcolm Ross: Caretaker of CanLit." *Quill and Quire* (May 1978): 21–22.

Solecki, Sam, ed. *Imagining Canadian Literature: The Selected Letters of Jack McClelland*. Toronto: Key Porter Books, 1998.

Staines, David. Introduction. *The Impossible Sum of Our Traditions: Reflections on Canadian Literature*, by Malcolm Ross. Toronto: McClelland and Stewart, 1986, 7–19.

Stevens, Peter. "Another Novel 18 Years Later." *Windsor Star*, 19 October 1974, p. 14.

Stewart, Sandy. *From Coast to Coast: A Personal History of Radio in Canada*. Toronto: CBC, 1985.

Stone, Tamara. "A Memoir of My Mother." In *We Who Can Fly: Poems, Essays and Memories in Honour of Adele Wiseman*. Ed. Elizabeth Greene. Dunvegan: Cormorant Books, 1997, 41–43.

Stouck, David. *As for Sinclair Ross*. Toronto: University of Toronto Press, 2005.

___. *Ethel Wilson: A Critical Biography*. Toronto: University of Toronto Press, 2003.

Studies in Canadian Literature 25, 1 (2000). Special issue on Canadian Literature and the Business of Publishing.

Sullivan, Rosemary. *By Heart: Elizabeth Smart, A Life*. Toronto: Penguin Books Canada, 1991.

___. *The Red Shoes: Margaret Atwood Starting Out*. Toronto: HarperCollins, 1998.

___. *Shadow Maker: The Life of Gwendolyn MacEwen*. Toronto: HarperCollins, 1996.

Teleky, Richard. *Goodnight, Sweetheart and Other Stories*. Dunvegan: Cormorant Books, 1993.

___. *Hungarian Rhapsodies: Essays on Ethnicity, Identity, and Culture*. Seattle: University of Washington Press, 1997.

___. *Pack Up the Moon*. Toronto: Thomas Allen, 2001.

___. *The Paris Years of Rosie Kamin*. South Royalton: Steerforth Press, 1998.

Thacker, Robert. *Alice Munro, Writing Her Lives: A Biography*. Toronto: McClelland and Stewart, 2005.

Thomas, Audrey. *Blown Figures*. Vancouver: Talonbooks, 1974.

"Thorny Paths." Rev. of *The Sacrifice*, by Adele Wiseman; *Peter Perry*, by Michael Campbell; and *The Angel in the Corner*, by Monica Dickens. *Times Literary Supplement*, 9 November 1956, p. 661.

Toner, Patrick. *If I Could Turn and Meet Myself: The Life of Alden Nowlan*. Fredericton: Goose Lane Editions, 2000.

Van Luven, Lynne. "Books in Review." *Lethbridge Herald*, 23 December 1978, p. 46.

Wachtel, Eleanor. "Profile: Voice of the Prophet." *Books in Canada* (October 1984): 8–13.

Waddington, Miriam. *Apartment Seven: Essays Selected and New*. Studies in Canadian Literature. Toronto: Oxford University Press, 1989.

Weaver, Robert. "Readers' Club Selection." *Canadian Reader* 15, 10 [December 1974]: 2–3.

Weinzweig, Helen. *Basic Black with Pearls*. Toronto: House of Anansi Press, 1980.

West, James L.W., III. *American Authors and the Literary Marketplace since 1900*. Philadelphia: University of Pennsylvania Press, 1988.

Whiteman, Bruce. "The Archive of the Macmillan Company of Canada Ltd. Part I: 1905–1965." *Library Research News* [McMaster University Library] 8, 1 (Spring 1984).

___. *Lasting Impressions: A Short History of English Publishing in Quebec*. Montréal: Véhicule Press, 1994.

____, Charlotte Stewart, and Catherine Funnell. *A Bibliography of Macmillan of Canada Imprints 1906–1980*. Toronto: Dundurn Press, 1985.

Windeyer, Kendal. "Old Hand Tries Again." *Gazette* [Montreal], 5 October 1974, p. 55.

Wiseman, Adele. "A Brief Anatomy of an Honest Attempt at a Pithy Statement about the Impact of the Manitoba Environment on My Development as an Artist." *Mosaic* 3, 3 (Spring 1970): 98–106.

____. *Crackpot*. Toronto: McClelland and Stewart, 1974.

____. "Drunken Hero Fails His Modern Cinderella." Rev. of *A Casual Affair: A Modern Fairytale*, by Sylvia Fraser. *Toronto Star*, 11 March 1978, p. D7.

____. "Duel in the Kitchen." *Maclean's* (7 January 1961): 22–23+. Rpt. as "On Wings of Tongue" in *Canadian Jewish Short Stories*. Ed. Miriam Waddington. Toronto: Oxford University Press, 1990, 139–52.

____. "Excerpts from 'The Lovebound: A Tragi-Comedy.'" *Journal of Canadian Fiction* 31–32 (1981): 140–47.

____. "Fanfare by Ronald [sic; in fact Roland] Penner." *Westerner: Truth and Justice for the West* [Winnipeg], 28 June 1947, p. 10; 5 July 1947, p. 10; 12 July 1947, p. 10; 19 July 1947, p. 10; 2 August 1947, p. 10; 9 August 1947, p. 10; 16 August 1947, p. 10; 23 August 1947, p. 10; 30 August 1947, p. 10; 6 September 1947, p. 10; 13 September 1947, p. 10.

____. "From *Crackpot*." *Canadian Writing Today*. Ed. Mordecai Richler. Harmondsworth: Penguin, 1970, 233–45.

____. "Goon of the Moon and the Expendables." *Malahat Review* 98 (March 1992): 5–44.

____. "How to Go to China." *Chinada: Memoirs of the Gang of Seven*, by Gary Geddes, Geoff Hancock, Robert Kroetsch, Patrick Lane, Alice Munro, Suzanne Paradis, and Adele Wiseman. Dunvegan: Quadrant Press, 1982, 98–128.

____. *Kenji and the Cricket*. Illus. Shizuye Takashima. Erin: Porcupine's Quill, 1988.

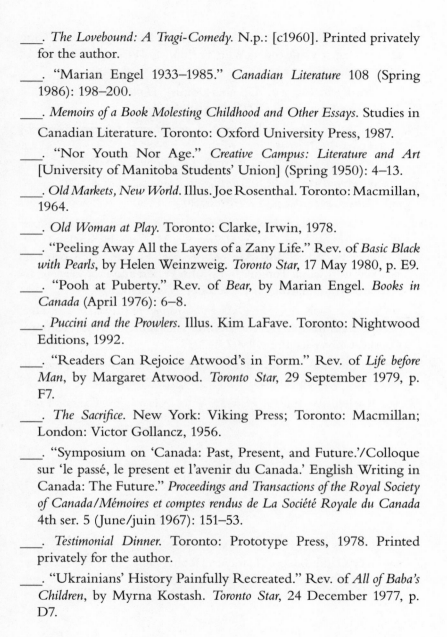

___. *The Lovebound: A Tragi-Comedy*. N.p.: [c1960]. Printed privately for the author.

___. "Marian Engel 1933–1985." *Canadian Literature* 108 (Spring 1986): 198–200.

___. *Memoirs of a Book Molesting Childhood and Other Essays*. Studies in Canadian Literature. Toronto: Oxford University Press, 1987.

___. "Nor Youth Nor Age." *Creative Campus: Literature and Art* [University of Manitoba Students' Union] (Spring 1950): 4–13.

___. *Old Markets, New World*. Illus. Joe Rosenthal. Toronto: Macmillan, 1964.

___. *Old Woman at Play*. Toronto: Clarke, Irwin, 1978.

___. "Peeling Away All the Layers of a Zany Life." Rev. of *Basic Black with Pearls*, by Helen Weinzweig. *Toronto Star*, 17 May 1980, p. E9.

___. "Pooh at Puberty." Rev. of *Bear*, by Marian Engel. *Books in Canada* (April 1976): 6–8.

___. *Puccini and the Prowlers*. Illus. Kim LaFave. Toronto: Nightwood Editions, 1992.

___. "Readers Can Rejoice Atwood's in Form." Rev. of *Life before Man*, by Margaret Atwood. *Toronto Star*, 29 September 1979, p. F7.

___. *The Sacrifice*. New York: Viking Press; Toronto: Macmillan; London: Victor Gollancz, 1956.

___. "Symposium on 'Canada: Past, Present, and Future.'/Colloque sur 'le passé, le present et l'avenir du Canada.' English Writing in Canada: The Future." *Proceedings and Transactions of the Royal Society of Canada/Mémoires et comptes rendus de La Société Royale du Canada* 4th ser. 5 (June/juin 1967): 151–53.

___. *Testimonial Dinner*. Toronto: Prototype Press, 1978. Printed privately for the author.

___. "Ukrainians' History Painfully Recreated." Rev. of *All of Baba's Children*, by Myrna Kostash. *Toronto Star*, 24 December 1977, p. D7.

____. "Where Learning Means Hope: Hong Kong's Canadian Club Does What It Can to Aid Worthy Pupils." *Weekend Magazine*, 18 May 1963, p. 18+.

____. "Writing in Ontario: Up and Doing." *Hungry Mind Review: A Midwestern Book Review* 10 (Spring 1989): 8.

[Wiseman, Adele.] Business Personal advertisement. *Telegram* [Toronto] 28 January 1961, p. 46.

____, ed. *Stepney Jester* [London] 1951; July 1956.

Wisse, Ruth R. *The Modern Jewish Canon: A Journey through Language and Culture.* New York: Free Press, 2000.

Woodcock, George. "Books. Adele Wiseman and Sinclair Ross: Return Engagements." Rev. of *Sawbones Memorial*, by Sinclair Ross; *Crackpot*, by Adele Wiseman; *Stories from Ontario*, sel. Germaine Warkentin; *Violence in the Arts*, by John Fraser; and *Exxoneration*, by Richard Rohmer. *Maclean's* (October 1974): 110.

____. "Weaver, Robert." *The Oxford Companion to Canadian Literature.* Second edition. Ed. Eugene Benson and William Toye. Toronto: Oxford University Press, 1997, 1172.

Wyatt, Louise. "A Memorable Encounter." *London Free Press*, 16 December 1978, p. B4.

Wyatt, Rachel. *Crackpot: A Play.* Toronto: Playwrights Canada Press, 1995.

INDEX